PRAISE FOR AI· PEDAGOGY

"This is an outstanding and necessary book from an inspirational educator. AI is here, as Wathall clearly shows, and we cannot turn back the clocks even if we wanted to. But this book shows we should not want to because there are so many possibilities to make education better, easier, more exciting and more suited to the future. This is full of ideas and examples from policy making and ethics to lesson planning and assessment that will take any teacher or school leader forward in their understanding and their practice."

Chris Binge, MA Cantab
International Education Consultant
Former Leader of International Schools

"A must read for any school leaders looking to create or re-visit their AI or digital literacy policy. Wathall demonstrates once again that she is keeping ahead of the curve as education evolves around us. Her latest work is the perfect mix of up-to-date knowledge, practical advice and resources, and of maintaining a focus on the heart of the discussion of how to use AI responsibly and effectively. We all know that we need to embrace AI as a tool, this book shows us how."

Christian Chiarenza
HS Assistant Principal, Fukuoka International School

"A timely book that not only compels educators to take action now but also equips teachers and school leaders with the tools and language to embrace AI-Powered Pedagogy in their schools. Wathall succeeds in connecting the dots between an ethical school-wide approach, empathy for the learning journey of all educators and of the learner, coupled with inspirational examples. Her passion for ensuring AI serves as a collaborative learning partner in every classroom and is utilized as a force for good makes this a must-read for anyone working in education today. Wow!"

Aubrey Curran
International Education Consultant, Trainer & Coach
Former Head of School

"A book to support the systemic approach to AI for schools in a time when many are feeling overwhelmed, thank you. The focus on the human centered education empowered by the tools at hand is both hopeful and inspiring. Wathall has provided a resource that can impact everything from macro policy to micro individual practice and the examples really drive home the idea that it really is all about pedagogy and learning at the heart, as it always has been. Education is a human centered endeavour that can become even more learning focused by utilizing AI tools to save time and focus on what's most powerful for learning."

Dr Michael Johnston
CEO SJI International School

"This book could not be a more timely and helpful contribution to the conversation so many of us are having about the impact of AI on the world of education. What I love about Jennifer's offering is the clear and unapologetic focus on pedagogy. By positioning AI *in service* of learning – rather than a threat to teaching, the agency and pedagogical repertoire of educators becomes more rather than less important. This is an empowering and enlightening book and one every teacher should have in their collection!"

Kath Murdoch
Author and International Consultant in Education

"One of my favourite sections is "The Four Stages of AI-Powered Pedagogy Adoption," which emphasizes leveraging technological advancements to achieve otherwise impossible results rather than merely replacing classroom tools. This approach aligns with the paradigm shift Wathall describes, providing practical steps for integrating AI into lessons. It's clear, jargon-free message makes it an easy, interesting and powerful read."

David Panford-Quainoo
DP Physics, Math and TOK Teacher

"AI-Powered Pedagogy" by Dr. Jennifer Chang Wathall is a must-read guide for educators and educational leaders looking to effectively and responsibly incorporate AI into their schools and teaching practice. It offers a comprehensive framework for creating institution-wide AI policies, emphasizing ethical considerations, privacy, and collaboration.

Jennifer also empowers teachers by highlighting strategies to automate administrative tasks and enhance student engagement, while focusing on learner-centric AI applications. These promote concept and inquiry based learning with a strong emphasis on ethics and academic integrity. I found great value in the practical tips, real-life examples, and case studies scattered throughout.

In the rapidly developing world of AI, it's easy to feel overwhelmed. Jennifer's book offers a comprehensive understanding of the current AI landscape in education and provides enduring principles to hold on to."

Jan-Mark Seewald
Education Consultant
Former Assistant Head of School

"From the very first pages of her book, Wathall pictures a future of education that sets the bar high for rest of the book. And she reaches that bar. It is a book not only about using AI to enhancing teachers' workflow, it is a book not only about making existing learning better, it is a book about transforming education.

In Wathall's future of education, technology is used to extend human capabilities into unthinkable directions. The book is written for teachers and school leaders, covering all AI-related aspects, from principles to policy writing to pedagogy. It contains specific examples, that any teacher can use from tomorrow in their work. The big ideas are structured in diagrams and flow charts making everything easy to understand and to remember. The book is a must for any school that looks into the future."

Dr Daniela Vasile
Director of Learning, Avenor College

AI-POWERED PEDAGOGY

REDEFINING EDUCATION

AI-POWERED PEDAGOGY

REDEFINING EDUCATION

DR. JENNIFER CHANG WATHALL

Foreword by Alexis Wiggins

ISBN 978-988-70646-8-8
Published by Jennifer Chang Wathall
Hong Kong

Cover Image

Generated by Dall-E-3

Prompt: Can you create a black and white sketch of Harmonising AI and Human Input

DISCLAIMER: This book may direct you to access third-party content via web links, QR codes, or other scannable technologies, which are provided for your reference by the author. The author makes no guarantee that such third-party content will be available for your use and encourages you to review the terms and conditions of such third-party content. The author takes no responsibility and assumes no liability for your use of any third-party content, nor does the author approve, sponsor, endorse, verify, or certify, such third-party content.

CONTENTS

LIST OF FIGURES

Chapter 5

Chapter 6

Chapter 8

Chapter 10

FOREWORD
BY ALEXIS WIGGINS

I met Jennie years ago when we both worked separately as consultants and workshop leaders for the IB. At the time, she was focused on concept-based teaching in mathematics, and I was working on the DP's Approaches to Teaching and Learning. We had an instant connection. I remember hearing about her impact on math in the IBDP program, and I immediately went and read some of the math writing she had done for the IB. I was fascinated; I wish my math education had been taught conceptually within larger frameworks like "Patterns"; it would have been so much more meaningful to this student of the humanities!

My father, the late education reformer Grant Wiggins, instilled in me a passion for pedagogy and a drive for teaching for deep, lasting understanding. He would have loved Jennie and her approach to teaching and learning: always focused on conceptual understanding and the "big ideas."

Although Jennie and I live half a world apart, I've followed her career admiringly over the years, reading her newsletters, happily bumping into her at conferences, and watching her insightful videos. She is a wealth of information on all things education, which is why I'm thrilled she's come out with *AI-Powered Pedagogy*.

I straddle three different education worlds in my current work - classroom teacher, school leader, and consultant. In all three of these arenas, my job has become infinitely more complex because of the pace at which AI is advancing. It can feel like a roller coaster of existential dread and creative excitement over and over again, even just within the same afternoon.

As a high school English teacher, my team and I are constantly trying to stay ahead of the curve so that we can offer our students the best opportunities for growth while still ensuring academic integrity, no small feat with the breathless innovations of AI right now. As the Director for Teaching and Learning at my pre-K-12 independent school in the Houston, TX area, I have had to pivot to focus much of my time on the pedagogical, technical, and legal implications of AI in order to help draft evergreen AI guidelines for our school community, something that can take a lot of time and energy to get right. And as a consultant, I've had calls from schools all over the U.S. wanting guidance and workshops for teachers on how to grapple with AI and assessment in the classroom; surprisingly, there are few answers or experts out there to turn to, and even fewer books on the subject right now.

Jennie's book could not come at a better time for me; it does not paint a doomsday scenario in which we have to return to a tech-free environment to ensure learning is happening, nor is it Pollyanna in its approach to dealing with the very real challenges of AI in schools. In Jennie's words, it's about "enabling innovation, empowering teachers, and enhancing humanity" at a moment of great excitement and uncertainty.

AI-Powered Pedagogy is the book you want to help you make sense of how AI will impact your job and students' lives. It gives me great comfort to know that Jennie is leading the way, lighting the path for us, because she has always been full of both practical steps and deep wisdom.

I know I'll be referring to this book often in the coming months (and years!) for all of my roles, and I know I'll be a better teacher, school leader, and consultant as a result.

Alexis Wiggins

Author of *The Best Class You Never Taught: How Spider Web Discussion Can Turn Students into Learning Leaders* and Director of the Cohort of Educators for Essential Learning

PREFACE

Welcome to *AI-Powered Pedagogy*, a comprehensive guide designed to empower you—the educator—with the knowledge, tools, and confidence to integrate artificial intelligence (AI) into your teaching practices effectively. The main focus of this book is to provide you with practical strategies and tools to navigate the exciting, ever-changing AI landscape.

Why Did I Write This Book?

While the concept of artificial intelligence has been around for decades, its application in education only began to capture mainstream attention in the last couple of years with the initial release of OpenAI's ChatGPT in November 2022.

Integrating AI into various sectors has not only revolutionized business practices but also shown immense potential to enhance educational methodologies. Several compelling statistics from a few sources underscore the growing pervasiveness of AI:

- 75% of knowledge workers use AI at work today (Microsoft, 2024).
- 90% of workers report AI helps them save time, 85% report they can focus on their most important work, 84% report they can be more creative, and 83% enjoy their work more (Microsoft, 2024).
- 66% of industry leaders report they wouldn't employ someone without AI skills (Microsoft, 2024).

- 71% of industry leaders say they'd rather employ a less experienced candidate with AI skills than a more experienced candidate without them (Microsoft, 2024).
- 73% of US businesses incorporate AI into some facets of their operations (PwC, 2023).
- 54% of companies had adopted generative AI in their operations by November 2023—just one year after the release of ChatGPT (PwC, 2023).
- Two-thirds of jobs could see partial automation through AI. However, many of these jobs will be augmented by AI, not replaced (Goldman Sachs, 2023),
- After its launch in November 2022, ChatGPT quickly amassed over a million users in just five days and reached 100 million users in under two months, becoming the fastest-growing consumer app at that time—a record later surpassed by Facebook's Threads app (Statista, 2023).
- Businesses implementing AI technologies are projected to see an average revenue increase of between 6% and 10% (Statista, 2023).
- 46% of American companies report savings ranging from $25,000 to $70,000 through their use of ChatGPT (Statista, 2023).
- Current AI technologies can automate tasks that currently take up 60% to 70% of a worker's time (McKinsey, 2023).
- Data management roles are expected to be significantly affected by AI, with about 90% of data processing and 80% of data collection jobs projected to be automated through the use of generative AI (Statista, 2023).

These statistics not only illustrate the rapid adoption and economic impact of AI across industries but also provide a strong rationale for exploring its potential in education. In this book, I explore into how these transformative technologies can be harnessed to enrich teaching methods, enhance learning experiences, and prepare both educators and students for a future where AI is ubiquitous. As AI becomes more deeply integrated into our educational landscape and lives, we must prioritize the development of robust pedagogy and a framework for ethical academic integrity.

The reason for writing a book on AI-powered pedagogy stems from the need to bridge the gap between the potential of AI in education and its practical, effective implementation in classrooms. While the excitement around AI's capabilities is palpable, many educators lack clear guidance on how to integrate these tools into their teaching practices meaningfully.

I posed the following overarching questions to guide the development of the concepts in this book:

- How do institutional frameworks support innovation and integrity in AI?
- How can we enhance teacher agency through effective AI integration, saving time and streamlining workflow?
- How can AI-powered pedagogy develop the ethical and humanistic learner?

This book aims to give educators a framework and actionable strategies for harnessing AI to enhance learning experiences, moving beyond the mere use of AI for the personalization of learning, which I think is just the glorified individual transmission of knowledge. While AI is often used for personalizing learning, I believe it's important to focus on how AI can help develop essential human qualities such as creativity, curiosity, and wonderment while fostering a sense of community among learners.

How Did I Write This Book?

When writing this book on AI-powered pedagogy, I found invaluable thought partners in bots I subscribe to on Poe.com. These included GPT-4, Gemini 1.5 Pro, Claude-3-Opus, GPT-4-128k, and GPT-4o, to name a few. This collaboration was not just about leveraging an AI tool; it was about engaging in a dynamic exchange of ideas, where a given bot served as both a sounding board and a source of inspiration. I began by using the design thinking process to steer the creation of this book, guiding me through a process that begins with a deep empathy for our readers—educators like you. My journey started with the Empathize stage, where I sought to genuinely understand the challenges, aspirations, and nuances of incorporating AI into educational settings.

Throughout the writing process, I interacted with different bots much like a co-author, posing questions, challenging their outputs, and refining their suggestions. This iterative dialogue helped to deepen the content, providing diverse perspectives and insights that only a machine learning model, trained on a vast text database, could offer. Bots also served as my first line editor, refining my expressions and clarifying my messaging and communication, and I was able to compare different bots' responses through the platform Poe.com easily.

Using AI in writing the book exemplified the very principles of AI-powered pedagogy that this book itself discusses. It shows how AI can support creative endeavors, making my ideas clearer and more understandable. By utilizing various AI tools, I explored and synthesized long documents about future educational trends with greater confidence (for example, AI tools such as ChatPDF or AI Assistant in Adobe Acrobat). The AI's ability to generate text based on specified prompts let me conduct my initial research effectively and efficiently. This partnership underscored the potential of AI as a transformative tool for writing, editing, and streamlining the content creation process, ultimately enriching the quality and precision of my final output.

Human input is a fundamental principle in any AI integration, and I was thrilled to have Stacey, my trusted and highly experienced proofreader, lend her invaluable human touch to the proofreading and editing of this book.

My Journey Through Design Thinking

This book is the culmination of extensive research (using AI tools to summarize, such as AI Assistant in Adobe Acrobat), extensive interviews (educators I know), and detailed online surveys, all framed around the design thinking process to ensure that the content is not only informative but also deeply aligned with the needs and wants of educators today.

I consider myself incredibly fortunate to have met Marcus Lui back in our university days. Not only is he a dear friend, but he's also an industry expert regarding design thinking. The hours we spent together brainstorming and bouncing ideas off each other truly opened my eyes to the art of understanding and solving problems creatively. Marcus excels at delving into users' minds and synthesizing insights from qualitative data. His passion for design thinking helped me see the world through a designer's lens.

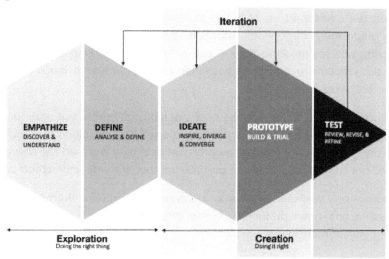

Designing for Learners' Agency:
The Design Thinking Framework

Iteration

| EMPATHIZE | DEFINE | IDEATE | PROTOTYPE | TEST |
| DISCOVER & UNDERSTAND | ANALYSE & DEFINE | INSPIRE, DIVERGE & CONVERGE | BUILD & TRIAL | REVIEW, REVISE, & REFINE |

Exploration
Doing the right thing

Creation
Doing it right

Adapted from Hasso-Plattner School of Design (d.school), Stanford University Marcus Lui and Dr Jennifer Chang Wathall

Empathizing with Educators

Design thinking steered the creation of this book, guiding me through an iterative process that began with a deep empathy for my readers—educators like you. My journey started with the Empathize stage, where I sought to genuinely understand the challenges, aspirations, and nuances of incorporating AI into educational settings.

To gather authentic insights and diverse perspectives, I interviewed a broad range of educators, from primary school teachers to university professors, each bringing unique experiences and expectations regarding AI in education. These conversations allowed us to explore the practical realities, hopes, and concerns that educators face daily.

This empathetic approach provided a foundation of real-world insights that shaped the subsequent stages of Define, Ideate, Prototype, and Test, which culminated in the birth of this book.

Using AI tools to IDEATE

One of the ways I commonly use AI in my classroom is to support students with ideation and communication, particularly for those who are English language learners or need additional support. I've developed an AI bot in Poe, https://poe.com/PanfordsAssistant designed to gently guide them through the ideation stages of their projects. Since I began explicitly discussing with my students how to use AI ethically—to refine and enhance their creativity rather than replace it—they have wholeheartedly embraced it, leading to significantly fewer instances of plagiarism.

One student, in particular, shared how transformative this bot was for her, especially in developing her ideas for the Theory of Knowledge (TOK) exhibition. She told me, "It really helps me to bring my thoughts to life," a comment that truly warmed my heart. This has not only boosted her confidence but also reassured her that she was understood and supported.

Witnessing my students overcome barriers and express themselves more freely and articulately has been profoundly rewarding, fostering a more supportive and inclusive learning environment in our classroom.

David Panford-Quainoo | DP Physics, Math and TOK Teacher

How Is This Book Structured?

In the realm of AI-powered pedagogy, three critical actors play pivotal roles in shaping the educational landscape: the institution, the educator, and the learner. The book is structured in three parts as such:

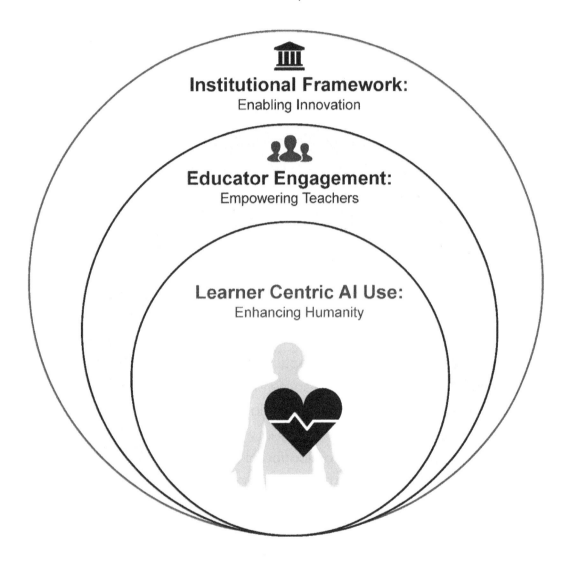

Part 1 sets the stage by providing the necessary resources and policies to enable the successful integration of AI technologies from an institutional perspective. Part 2 centers on educators, as the primary facilitators of learning, who must be empowered with the knowledge, skills, and tools to harness the potential of AI effectively in their teaching practices. Finally, Part 3 discusses the learners who are at the heart of this transformative approach, as AI-powered pedagogy aims to enhance their learning experiences and equip them with the competencies needed for success in an increasingly digital world. This section focuses on developing the ethical learner, helping them to integrate and use AI responsibly, and exploring how AI can enhance human qualities such as empathy.

By exploring the perspectives and roles of these three actors, this book provides a comprehensive understanding of how AI can be leveraged to revolutionize education at all levels.

Within the pages of this book, you will also find these additional resources:

- Guiding Questions: Each chapter begins with a guiding question that sets the stage for the discussions and explorations that follow.
- Practical Tips: Throughout the chapters, practical tips are highlighted by a lightbulb icon, offering actionable advice and insights.
- Printable Resources: Within some chapters, you'll find resources that can be printed for non-commercial use. These are designed to be used directly with your students or within your school community to reinforce learning and application of concepts.
- Discussion Questions: At the conclusion of each chapter, a set of discussion questions is provided. These are ideal for use in book study groups or as reflective prompts to deepen understanding of the material.
- Artefact Opportunities: These are practical suggestions for creating artefacts that help you apply your learning.

Who Is This Book For?

AI-Powered Pedagogy is crafted for a diverse audience within the educational sector. Here are key groups that will find this book particularly beneficial:

- K-12 Educators: For teachers in primary and secondary schools looking to enhance their classroom with AI-driven tools, this book offers practical strategies for integration, making sure that technology adoption aligns with educational standards and enhances learning outcomes.
- Higher Education Faculty: Professors and academic instructors will find advanced applications of AI that can support research and assessment at the tertiary level.
- Educational Administrators: School leaders and administrators will discover insights on implementing AI at a systemic level, ensuring that infrastructure, policy, and training support effective adoption.
- Instructional Designers and Technologists: Professionals focused on developing curriculum and educational technology will gain from detailed cases and innovative uses of AI in course design and student engagement.
- Student Teachers and Educators in Training: Emerging educators can use this book to stay ahead in the rapidly evolving educational landscape and be prepared to use AI tools effectively in their future classrooms.

As we investigate the specifics of AI applications, ethical considerations, practical case studies, and future trends, I invite you to join me in exploring the exciting intersection of AI and pedagogy, equipped with the tools to make a significant impact in your educational environment.

ACKNOWLEDGMENTS

In my journey of both personal and professional learning and growth, I've discovered a valuable secret: surround yourself with brilliant people.

I would like to express my gratitude to my brilliant husband, Ken Wathall, who is not only my life partner but also walks alongside me on this journey of life through all the ups and downs. You are my rock and my greatest supporter, always there to lift me up and encourage me. Your unwavering love and dedication inspire me every day, and I am incredibly lucky to have you by my side. Thank you for being my constant source of strength, joy, and unconditional love.

Thank you, brilliant Marcus Lui, for your friendship, for helping me to grow and learn intellectually, and for getting me through our university days in the 1980s. I am eternally grateful for your unwavering support and wisdom and the countless memories we have created.

ABOUT THE AUTHOR

Dr. Jennifer Chang-Wathall is an independent educational consultant, author, and part-time instructor at the University of Hong Kong. With a rich background spanning over 30 years in international education, she has worked at various international schools, such as South Island School and Island School in Hong Kong, and The United Nations International School in New York.

In the international arena, she has presented numerous keynote addresses and workshops about concept-based mathematics, concept-based curriculum and instruction, and educational technology to Pre-K-12 educators. Based on her master's and doctorate in educational technology, she regularly facilitates professional learning on the innovative use of digital instructional tools and, more recently, AI-powered pedagogy. She has created numerous online courses and remains at the forefront of incorporating educational technology, using effective pedagogical practices to improve learning outcomes.

Jennifer is a certified trainer in the DiSC® behavior assessment tool and a certified independent consultant in *Concept-Based Curriculum and Instruction for the Thinking Classroom* by Dr. H. Lynn Erickson. Her consultancy work is dedicated to collaborating with departments and educational institutions to shift their focus toward deep conceptual understanding and inquiry-based learning. Additionally, she uses her certification as a performance coach to support educational transitions and change.

She co-authored several student reference books for the IB Diploma Mathematics courses published by Oxford University Press. Her bestselling book, *Concept-Based Mathematics: Teaching for Deep Understanding in Secondary Schools*, has significantly influenced secondary mathematics education.

AUTHOR'S NOTE

From an early age, I have always been driven by a curiosity to learn and grow, a trait that was fostered by my late father, David Kuo Cheng Chang. There's something truly exciting about leading and embracing new innovative tools that can transform how we teach and learn. My passion for these innovations isn't just about the novelty of digital tools (even though I love every shiny new ball I come across!); it's deeply rooted in my commitment to enriching the learning journeys of students. It's about ensuring that we are harnessing every possible resource to create better experiences for learners in all contexts.

I'm what's called an *early adopter*—I always found myself fascinated by new technologies, from the graphical display calculator (GDC) in the late 1990s to the interactive whiteboards in the early 2000s, and I participated in the launch of the first 1:1 program in Hong Kong in the mid-2000s. I have always loved exploring new innovative digital tools with the ultimate goal of enhancing learning for students. This led me to pursue my master's and doctorate in educational technology, researching professional learning frameworks for the online environment. I majored in pure and applied mathematics for my undergraduate degree, so I've also had a lifelong passion for mathematics teaching and learning.

It was an immense privilege to serve as a former classroom teacher for 27 years, a role that gave me rich and invaluable experiences. Since 2007, I have had the honor of collaborating with educators globally, focusing on professional learning and growth. These partnerships have not only broadened my perspective but have also deepened my commitment to cultivating curiosity, promoting lifelong learning, and nurturing a love of learning for the sake of learning with adults, teenagers, and children.

*I dedicate this book in loving memory of my father,
David Kuo-Cheng Chang (1929–2014),
who inspired me to be a lifelong learner*

*and my mother,
Chih-Mei Chang, who I am in awe of every day
for her energy, positivity, and joie de vivre.*

PART 1
INSTITUTIONAL FRAMEWORKS: ENABLING INNOVATION
HOW DO INSTITUTIONAL FRAMEWORKS SUPPORT INNOVATION AND INTEGRITY?

Image generated by DALL·E 3, 2024

CHAPTER 1
INTRODUCTION

*It is clear that we are at an inflection point
in the history of humanity.*
—Mustafa Suleyman, artificial intelligence (AI) entrepreneur

What's All the AI Buzz About?

It's pretty amazing to think about how much artificial intelligence (AI) has already become a part of our everyday lives. We are just beginning to learn that we interact with AI more often than we realized—like when social media apps use facial recognition technology to automatically suggest tagging someone we know in the pictures we post. Other examples are when our email services filter out spam and prioritize important messages, ensuring we see what matters most, or when our streaming services recommend the perfect movie for our Friday night. AI has been working for years behind the scenes, using data from our past interactions to make these personalized suggestions.

In fact, AI has completely permeated every aspect of our lives. Consider self-driving vehicles that navigate our roads with increasing autonomy, or artists who collaborate with AI image generators to explore new creative horizons and develop unique forms of art. Similarly, in the agricultural sector, farmers in rural areas leverage AI to optimize every aspect of farming—from planting to harvesting. This technology ensures that crops are grown more efficiently and sustainably.

In the rapidly advancing world of healthcare, AI robots are dramatically transforming medical practices in previously inconceivable ways. Robotic assistants are increasingly being used in surgery, enhancing precision and improving patient outcomes significantly. My brother, Dr. Tim Chang, a leading robotic surgeon, is particularly excited about AI's role in robotic-assisted surgeries. He highlighted how AI-enabled systems are revolutionizing

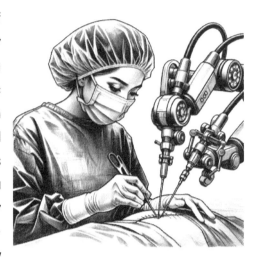

Image generated by DALL·E 3, 2024

healthcare by enabling greater accuracy and less invasive procedures, resulting in significantly shorter recovery times for patients. In short, these AI-enabled systems enhance image analysis and improve hand movements to ensure no tremors, making surgery more precise and accurate, leading to less tissue trauma. In the future AI may enhance surgical planning by superimposing radiological scans in live surgery, making real-time adjustments based on the patient's unique anatomy. AI may also identify critical structures to optimize techniques, leading to more accurate treatments and faster recoveries.

AI's contributions also extend into the arenas of public welfare, where algorithms are being employed to enhance disaster response strategies, providing critical data that helps mitigate the impacts of natural disasters. The role of AI extends beyond just simplifying tasks; it enhances them, boosting efficiency and making advanced capabilities more accessible across various fields and industries.

> **AI in Education**
>
> As a teacher, I've found AI to be an invaluable aid in managing essential yet time-consuming administrative tasks. This includes modifying assessments for students who need extra support, creating detailed notes on specific physics problems, and developing both similar and extension questions related to the content. By using it for these tasks, I can devote more time to direct engagement with my students, deepening my understanding of their needs and enhancing the guidance I provide throughout their learning journeys.
>
> The efficiency introduced by AI not only boosts my ability to meet diverse learning needs but also enriches the overall educational experience for my students and improves my, work-life balance. The integration of AI has significantly enhanced my effectiveness and productivity as a teacher—it's almost like having a personal assistant who is exceptionally capable, provided I give clear instructions on what needs to be accomplished.
>
> **David Panford-Quainoo | DP physics, math and TOK teacher**

I think we can all agree that AI is also rapidly transforming the realm of education. As someone deeply passionate about teaching and learning, I find myself continually excited by the revolutionary changes AI is bringing, not only to our work-life balance but also to our educational practices.

The impact of AI extends beyond just the technological tools themselves; it's fundamentally enhancing the way we work and teach. By automating routine tasks, AI empowers educators to focus more on productivity and creativity. This allows for the crafting of lessons that are not only academically rigorous but also highly engaging and motivating. My hope is that this leads to a shift toward more dynamic classroom interactions, where the emphasis is on developing deep conceptual understanding and enhancing critical thinking skills through an inquiry-based learning environment.

Imagine a history class where students can have a conversation with Dr. Martin Luther King or Cleopatra through any large language model (LLM). AI is enhancing interactive learning by enabling students to engage directly with historical figures through a simple interface. These AI tools use vast databases of historical texts, speeches, and documented behaviors to respond to student inquiries, providing a first-person perspective on historical events and decisions. This form of interactive learning not only makes history tangible and engaging but also allows students to develop a deeper understanding by asking questions, and receiving answers that are informed by historical data. Such immersive experiences can transform traditional learning, making it more engaging and informative by allowing students to explore history by talking to historical figures.

Image generated by DALL·E 3, 2024

In science education, AI can significantly enhance collaborative research projects by enabling students to work together on analyzing large-scale data sets, such as climate change trends. Leveraging the capabilities of LLMs, AI tools can quickly and efficiently process vast quantities of qualitative data, identifying patterns through thematic coding. This application of AI not only facilitates a deeper understanding of scientific concepts but also cultivates essential skills in data literacy and teamwork. By integrating AI tools, educators can provide students with valuable experience in handling big data, crucial for many scientific fields. This collaborative approach not only enriches the learning experience but also prepares students for future challenges in a data-driven world.

In social studies, AI tools can revolutionize the way debates on current events are structured and managed. By employing AI, educators can enhance the learning experience by providing students with resources, helping to structure arguments, and even evaluating debates based on various metrics such as clarity, use of evidence, and persuasion. This application of AI streamlines the organization of debates. It allows students to focus more on developing their critical thinking and argumentation skills, fostering a deeper understanding of the topics discussed and promoting a more interesting and productive learning environment.

In mathematics, AI can be utilized to enhance collaborative learning experiences by facilitating complex problem-solving challenges. For instance, AI can generate real-world scenarios that require open-ended mathematical solutions, such as optimizing logistics in a supply chain, designing cost-effective building plans, or even managing budgets for large projects. These scenarios can be set up as collaborative group activities, where students must apply various mathematical concepts like calculus, statistics, algebra, or geometry to solve practical problems. This approach helps students understand the applicability of mathematics to authentic real-life situations and also encourages teamwork, as they must work together to come up with solutions.

Another exciting application of AI in the education realm is that it can open the doors to more dynamic interdisciplinary educational approaches, especially enhancing our capabilities to incorporate project-based learning (PBL). AI can support educators in designing complex, multi-layered projects that integrate various disciplines, providing students with a holistic approach to learning. For example, AI can assist in generating concept-based and inquiry-based projects that address one of the seventeen UN Sustainable Development Goals (SDGs), requiring students to apply skills from across the curriculum—combining science, technology, art, and mathematics, for example—to solve real-world challenges. This makes learning more enjoyable and emphasizes the interconnectedness of knowledge and skills in authentic contexts.

The transformative power of AI in education is undeniable. By integrating AI into various facets of education, we are witnessing a paradigm shift not just in how subjects are taught, but also in how students develop communication skills and engage with and synthesize information. From enabling direct interactions with historical figures to facilitating large-scale collaborative projects that tackle real-world problems, AI is redefining the boundaries of traditional education. These innovations are not merely about the automation of tasks but are fundamentally enhancing education by making learning more interactive, interdisciplinary, and interesting. As AI continues to evolve, it is set to further empower educators and learners by providing tools that can adapt to the diverse needs of students and ignite an even greater passion for learning, allowing every student to thrive and flourish.

This ongoing revolution in education through AI not only prepares students for future challenges but also inspires them to innovate and think critically, ensuring they are ready to thrive in a rapidly changing world. Being part of this dynamic field at such a transformative time is exhilarating. I look forward to seeing how continued advancements in AI further refine our pedagogical strategies and enrich our students' educational journeys. This shift in education isn't just about adopting new tools; it's about fundamentally redefining the essence of how we teach and learn.

Pedagogy Before Technology

While AI tools and other educational technology offer significant potential to enhance our lives and improve learning experiences for students, it is crucial to remember that these tools are inanimate objects, which are absent of intent or moral direction. Their impact is determined by how we, as humans, choose to use them.

For instance, consider the analogy of a builder with a hammer: if a builder comes to your house to fix your roof and inadvertently lodges a giant hole in your roof, we don't blame the hammer, but rather the person who created the gaping hole. Similarly, the responsibility lies with us to utilize AI digital tools ethically and responsibly, ensuring they serve the greater good of society and enrich our educational systems. As we integrate these advanced technologies into our learning environments, we must be mindful stewards, guiding their application to foster positive outcomes and prevent misuse.

Image generated by DALL·E 3, 2024

I want to stress the essence of successfully integrating AI into education is in employing it to spark curiosity while upholding the effective pedagogical principles outlined in this book. By focusing on the pedagogical application of AI, educators can design student-centered learning experiences that encourage exploration and questioning rather than mere transmission of information. This approach empowers educators and students to take control of their learning journey, using AI as a dynamic partner that facilitates deeper understanding and creativity.

Less Is More

When it comes to exploring new AI tools as educators, it's important to keep things simple. There's a ton of new tools popping up every day, and it's easy to get overwhelmed. Instead of trying to keep up with every new release, we're better off focusing on just a few tools and really getting to know them inside and out. This way, we can avoid feeling overwhelmed and make sure we're using these tools effectively in our classrooms to actually boost learning, rather than chasing after every new shiny ball (I'm often guilty of this!).

And remember:

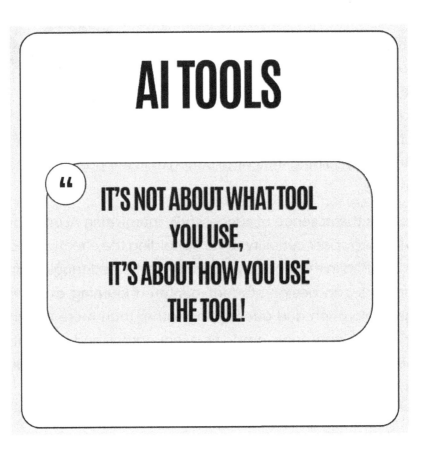

As educational institutions increasingly embrace AI to enhance teaching and learning, it is crucial to establish robust frameworks that enable innovation while ensuring responsible and effective implementation. Subsequent chapters will delve deeper into this topic, unpacking the complexities of integrating AI within educational settings and providing clear guidance and actionable steps to navigate this transformative journey effectively.

Before we begin our journey together, let me mention that I've purposely chosen not to focus on any particular AI tool; instead, the emphasis is placed on guiding principles, and strategies for effectively integrating AI into educational settings. However, to provide practical insights and examples, I will mention some AI tools that I have personally used and found useful in various contexts. For those interested in exploring AI tools further, I've compiled a detailed list of my current top fifty AI tools as of May 2024. This comprehensive list can be found in the appendix of the book, offering a handy reference to some of the most effective and innovative AI technologies I have found available for use in the education sector. Please note that as we are experiencing an unprecedented exponential growth in AI technology, my top fifty list will evolve accordingly.

In writing this book, I've also intentionally steered clear of the use of the dense jargon and complex technical language that often pervades computer science and programming texts. My focus is primarily on practical strategies that you, as an educator, can directly apply in your classroom. The essence of this book is to make the integration of AI into educational settings accessible, actionable, and beneficial for both you and your students. By demystifying AI and presenting its applications through clear, actionable examples, ideas for unit of inquiry, and classroom strategies, I aim to ensure that you can leverage the potential of AI-powered pedagogy without needing to use any underlying code or algorithmic complexities. This approach is designed to empower you to enhance your pedagogical methods and foster an enriching learning environment that harnesses the latest advancements in AI.

With that being said, while I try to avoid deep technical jargon, understanding some basic vocabulary can help in grasping the fundamental concepts of AI. So here are a few key terms verified by Wikipedia and Perplexity (which provided direct links to sources) and reworded by GPT-4:

Figure 1.1:

Ten AI Vocabulary Words

AI (artificial intelligence): The simulation of human intelligence in machines that are programmed to think like humans and mimic their actions. The term may also be applied to any machine that exhibits traits associated with a human mind in such communicating and problem-solving.

Bot (short for robot): a software application that is designed to automate certain tasks, often by interacting with users or other systems. Bots can be used for a variety of purposes, such as customer service, information gathering, or even social media interactions. A **chatbot** is a specific type of bot that is designed to engage in conversational interactions with users, typically through text-based interfaces. Chatbots use natural language processing and machine learning algorithms to understand and respond to user inputs.

Computer vision: A field of artificial intelligence that focuses on enabling computers to interpret and understand digital images and videos. It involves the development of algorithms and systems that can perform tasks such as object detection, image recognition, and scene understanding. Computer vision is used in a wide range of applications, including autonomous vehicles, medical imaging, and security systems. It relies on techniques such as deep learning and machine learning to analyze and make sense of visual data.

Generative AI: AI systems that can generate content, such as text, images, music, and more, through learning from large datasets to recognize patterns and structure. This type of AI can produce new outputs that are similar but not identical to the examples it has learned from. Generative AI models, such as GPT-3 and DALL·E, are trained on large datasets of existing content and can then use this knowledge to generate new, original content that mimics the style and characteristics of the training data. This can be used for a variety of applications, such as creative writing, music composition, and image generation.

GPT (generative pre-trained transformer): A type of large language model (LLM) that is trained on a vast amount of text data to generate human-like text. GPT models are known for their ability to produce coherent and contextually relevant text, making them useful for a variety of natural language processing tasks, such as language translation, text summarization, and question answering.

Hallucinations: AI-generated responses that present false or misleading information as fact, drawing a loose analogy with human hallucinations, which involve false perceptions.

Large language model (LLM): A type of artificial intelligence system that is trained on a vast amount of text data, allowing it to understand and generate human-like language. LLMs are characterized by their large size, often containing billions of parameters, and their ability to perform a wide range of natural language processing tasks, such as text generation, translation, and question answering. These models are employed in text generation, a subset of generative AI, where they generate text by sequentially predicting subsequent tokens or words after an initial input.

ML (machine learning): A field of artificial intelligence that focuses on the development of algorithms and statistical models that enable computers to perform specific tasks effectively without being explicitly programmed. ML systems learn from data, identifying patterns and making predictions or decisions based on that data

Neural Network: A type of machine learning model that is inspired by the structure and function of the human brain. It is composed of interconnected nodes, or "neurons," that can transmit signals to other neurons, allowing the network to learn and perform complex tasks, such as image recognition, natural language processing, and decision-making.

NLP (natural language processing): A field of artificial intelligence that focuses on the interaction between computers and human language. It involves the development of algorithms and systems that can understand, interpret, and generate human language, enabling computers to perform tasks such as language translation, text summarization, sentiment analysis, and question answering.

OK, I'm going to stop there, as I could've included hundreds more terms, but that is not the purpose of this book. I do hope that understanding these ten terms can provide some foundational vocabulary that helps in discussing and exploring AI applications in education and beyond.

Common Mistakes with AI Use

When integrating AI tools into educational institutions, it is crucial to avoid common pitfalls to ensure effective and ethical use.

Image generated by DALL·E 3, 2024

A dear friend recently shared a humbling experience from a demo lesson she conducted for an international school interview. She had used an LLM to generate math questions and answers, trusting it to deliver the correct content. However, mid-lesson, an astute student pointed out several incorrect answers. This unexpected wakeup call was a huge lesson for her, revealing that LLMs are often not factually correct.

My friend's experience emphasizes the importance of double-checking AI-generated content and highlighted a valuable lesson: while AI can be a powerful aid, it is essential to maintain a critical eye and verify information independently.

Institutions must establish protocols for double-checking AI-generated content. Studies show that chatbots powered by LLMs can produce inaccuracies and hallucinations, with up to 27% of responses containing random falsehoods and 46% presenting factual errors (Wikipedia, 2023). Ensuring that all AI-generated information is independently verified is critical to maintaining educational integrity. For further guidance on fact-checking, please refer to chapter 8.

Another frequent mistake with institutional AI use is emphasizing the technological features of new digital tools rather than focusing on how these tools can enhance pedagogy. I have attended many ed tech conferences that prioritize showcasing a large number of tools, often neglecting the pedagogical applications and implications of these tools. It's vital that educators prioritize the educational value and applications of technology over its novelty. This approach ensures that technology serves as a tool to support effective teaching strategies to enhance learning rather than overshadowing them.

Critical thinking is an essential skill in any educational endeavor, yet it is often neglected when using AI. Institutions must encourage educators to teach students not only to use AI but also to critically examine its outputs. This includes editing AI-generated content to ensure it makes sense.

Ethical dimensions of AI use must be at the forefront of institutional policies. Neglecting the ethical dimensions of AI use can result in decisions and actions that compromise student privacy, data security, and fairness. Educators and administrators must ensure that AI tools comply with ethical standards and legal regulations to protect students and maintain trust. This includes being vigilant about how student data is collected, stored, and used, ensuring transparency and consent are prioritized.

Academic integrity and honesty also play a critical role in the responsible use of AI in education. As AI becomes more prevalent in generating and curating content, students may rely too heavily on these tools, risking plagiarism or undermining their learning process. It is essential for institutions to instill a strong understanding of academic honesty in students, emphasizing the importance of original thought and integrity in their work when using AI-generated content.

Another pitfall is a lack of awareness about the biases and stereotypes that AI outputs can perpetuate. AI systems are only as unbiased as the data they are trained on, which can often include inherent societal prejudices. Recognizing and addressing these biases is crucial to prevent the reinforcement of stereotypes.

Institutions should guide educators and students to use AI tools without sacrificing authentic voice. While AI can generate content, it's crucial to edit for a genuine and personal touch. Over-reliance on AI can lead to the overuse of certain phrases like "profound," "tapestry," "threads," "woven," "harness," "delve," "vibrant," "landscape," "realm," "embark," and "vital," which can make writing sound generic and impersonal. Educators and students should be aware of these common AI-generated phrases and strive to maintain their own unique style and voice in their work. This list of overused AI words is not exhaustive but is compiled from research conducted by several bloggers and Reddit users, as well as my own experience. You will see I have tried to avoid these words in this book.

By addressing these issues, educators can better harness the potential of AI tools to enrich the learning environment while maintaining a high standard of education and critical engagement.

Figure 1.2 below gives a summary of some of the common mistakes with AI use.

Figure 1.2:

Common Mistakes with AI Use

6 MISTAKES WITH AI

1	NOT CHECKING FACTS: AI TOOLS HALLUCINATE
2	FOCUSING ON THE AI TOOL & NOT PEDAGOGY
3	NOT EDITING OUTPUT: DOES IT MAKE SENSE?
4	IGNORING ETHICS & ACADEMIC HONESTY
5	NOT RECOGNISING STEREOTYPES & BIAS
6	NOT INJECTING PERSONAL AUTHENTICITY

Practical Tip: Invite a working group that includes different members of the school community to co-create a list of common pitfalls associated with AI use. Transform this collective insight into a set of guidelines or protocols for the entire school community. By involving students and teachers in this process, you give them a sense of ownership and responsibility, which enhances the effectiveness of and adherence to these guidelines.

Professional Learning Opportunities for the School Community

Professional development is critical in ensuring that all stakeholders—educators, administrators, and policymakers—are well-prepared to leverage AI technologies in educational settings. It is imperative to provide training that simplifies AI concepts and illustrates practical applications within the classroom.

Professional learning opportunities should be designed to empower educators by providing them with the autonomy to choose learning pathways that align with their own interests and current expertise levels, aligning with andragogical principles. This empowerment is crucial in facilitating adult engagement and motivation, allowing educators to navigate the complexities of AI in a way that is personally and professionally enriching.

By enabling educators to tailor their learning experiences, a professional learning program can effectively address the diverse needs and capabilities of individual teachers. To foster community and a sense of teamwork and collaboration, I like to encourage forming interest-based professional learning groups, so educators can discuss and bounce ideas off each other.

Recognizing that professional growth is a continuous and sustained journey, it is recommended that professional development initiatives accommodate the varying stages of knowledge and experience among educators. Offering multiple entry points and a spectrum of learning modules catered to different levels of AI familiarity ensures that every educator, regardless of their starting point, has access to relevant and supportive educational opportunities. This inclusive approach helps to demystify AI for novices while providing more advanced insights for those with greater familiarity, thereby fostering a community of learning that values and supports continuous advancement.

Designing a Professional Learning Plan (PLP)

To ensure the development and implementation of the professional learning plan (PLP) are both teacher-centered and responsive, we anchor the process in *design thinking* principles. Figure 1.3 outlines the stages in the design thinking process.

By aligning the planning of professional learning with the design thinking process, we ensure that the program is not only systematic and well-structured but also deeply responsive to the needs of educators, fostering an environment conducive to effective learning and the practical application of AI in education.

Figure 1.3:

Design Thinking Stages

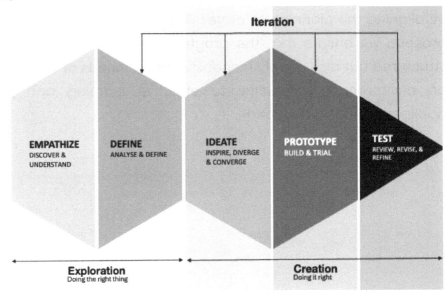

Designing for Learners' Agency:
The Design Thinking Framework

Adapted from Hasso-Plattner School of Design (d.school), Stanford University Marcus Lui and Dr Jennifer Chang Wathall

Here is a description of each step of the five-stage process for developing a PLP:

1. Empathize: Assess Needs and Set Goals

Begin by empathizing with your audience: members of the school community. The members of the school community include teachers, school administrators, parents, and students. Understand their current perceptions, challenges, and expectations regarding AI in education through surveys, interviews, and observations. This empathetic approach helps in accurately assessing the needs and readiness of teachers to adopt AI technologies. Use this information to define clear and tailored goals for the PLP that address the specific concerns and aspirations of the educators.

2. Define: Design the Professional Learning Opportunities

With an in-depth understanding of the community's needs and the goals of the program, clearly define what success looks like for the training. This involves structuring a program that takes into account varying levels of AI knowledge and aligns with the educational goals.

The program should be comprehensive, covering fundamental concepts of AI, practical applications in teaching, ethical considerations, and hands-on activities.

3. Ideate: Select Facilitators and Resources

In this creative, divergent phase, brainstorm and select the best possible resources, and facilitators who can deliver the training effectively. Consider various teaching aids, digital tools, expert speakers, and engaging materials that can enhance the learning experience.

Think innovatively about how to present complex AI concepts in a user-friendly manner that encourages active learning and participation. For example, each teacher could buddy up with another teacher to create an artefact based on their interest area and learning.

4. Prototype: Implement the Program

Treat the initial roll-out of the PLP as a prototype. Implement the planned sessions, workshops, and activities as designed, but remain open to making adjustments.

During this phase, it is crucial to maintain an iterative mindset, allowing for real-time changes based on ongoing feedback and observations.

5. Test: Evaluate and Iterate

Finally, rigorously test the effectiveness of the PLP by evaluating participant feedback, measuring learning outcomes, and observing the practical application of AI in classrooms.

Use this data to refine and improve the program. Consider this an iterative process where the program is continually enhanced and built upon based on teacher feedback and evolving needs.

Figure 1.4 summarizes this five-step process for designing a professional learning plan.

Figure 1.4:

Designing a Professional Learning Plan

DESIGNING A PROFESSIONAL LEARNING PLAN

1 **EMPATHIZE: ASSESS NEEDS AND SET GOALS**

Begin by empathizing with your audience, the educators, to understand their perceptions, challenges, and expectations around AI in education through surveys, interviews, and observations.

2 **DEFINE: DESIGN PROFESSIONAL LEARNING OPPORTUNITIES**

With an in-depth understanding of the teachers' needs and the goals of the program, clearly define what success looks like for the training. This involves structuring a program that takes into account varying levels of AI knowledge and aligns with the educational objectives.

3 **IDEATE: SELECT FACILITATORS AND RESOURCES**

In this creative divergent phase, brainstorm and select the best possible resources and facilitators who can deliver the training effectively.

4 **PROTOTYPE: IMPLEMENT THE PROGRAM**

Treat the initial roll-out of the professional learning program as a prototype. Implement the planned sessions, workshops, and activities as designed, but remain open to making adjustments.

5 **TEST: EVALUATE AND ITERATE**

Rigorously test the effectiveness of the program by evaluating participant feedback, measuring learning outcomes, and observing the practical application of AI in classrooms.

Here are some suggestions for professional learning topics that could be offered once this five-step process has been implemented:

1. AI-Powered Data Analytics for Education

Assess teachers' current knowledge of AI data analytics through surveys and interviews, and then design workshops covering AI fundamentals, practical data analysis applications, and ethical considerations. Implement sessions with hands-on practice and gather feedback to refine the program. Measure impact through surveys and student outcomes, making adjustments as needed.

2. AI for Administrative Efficiency

Survey staff to understand current administrative challenges, and set objectives to streamline operations with AI. Conduct workshops on AI applications for tasks like scheduling and resource management, gathering feedback to assess effectiveness. Measure impact through staff surveys and process efficiency assessments, adjusting as needed.

3. Ethical AI Use in Education

Survey students, teachers, and administrators to gauge understanding of AI ethics, and then plan sessions on ethical considerations, bias, and privacy. Implement workshops with practical insights and collect feedback to refine the program. Assess impact through feedback, policy compliance, and classroom observations, making necessary adjustments.

4. AI-Enhanced Curriculum Development

Determine teachers' needs and experiences with AI in curriculum design through surveys, and set goals to integrate AI effectively. Plan workshops covering AI tools for curriculum development and practical strategies, gathering feedback to improve sessions. Measure impact through teacher reflections and curriculum assessments, refining the training based on results.

Chapter Summary

This chapter introduced the transformative role of artificial intelligence (AI) across various sectors, highlighting its seamless integration into our daily lives. From predictive texting and AI-curated social media feeds to its applications in self-driving cars, creative industries, agriculture, and healthcare, AI's influence is pervasive and beneficial.

AI is also a revolutionary force in education, enhancing teaching methods and learning experiences. It can facilitate engaging historical interactions through conversations with historical figures and generate ideas for an interdisciplinary project-based learning (PBL) approach. The chapter discussed AI's benefits, highlighting its capability to augment collaborative and inquiry-based learning environments.

Despite the enthusiasm for AI, it is important to prioritize pedagogy over technological tool. Ethical use of AI tools and their alignment with educational goals are crucial to enhance learning rather than simply automate tasks.

Professional development for educators is essential for effective AI integration into teaching practices. A five-stage design thinking process was proposed for developing professional learning plans (PLPs) that cater to educators' needs, including empathizing with educators, defining success criteria, selecting resources, prototyping the program, and performing iterative testing.

The true potential of AI lies not in the tools themselves but in how they are utilized to expand human capabilities and improve quality of life. In education, AI is poised to revolutionize traditional teaching methods by making learning more interactive, engaging, and context based. This shift in pedagogy is not simply about adopting technology, but rethinking how teaching and learning occur.

Discussion Questions

1. Transformative Potential of AI: How do you perceive the role of AI in transforming traditional educational practices as described in the chapter? Discuss specific changes that AI could bring to your teaching area or subject.

2. Interdisciplinary Learning: AI is described as enhancing project-based learning (PBL) and interdisciplinary learning. Can you envision a project or lesson plan in your area that could integrate AI to foster a more holistic learning experience? How might AI facilitate the integration of different academic disciplines?

3. Role of Educators: As AI tools become more integrated into education, what do you think the evolving role of educators should be? How can teachers complement AI tools to enhance student learning rather than feel replaced by them?

4. Future of AI in Education: Based on the advancements discussed, what are your predictions or concerns for the future of AI in education? How do you think these changes will affect your teaching practices and your students' learning experiences in the next decade?

Artefact Opportunities

Explore AI in Everyday Life:

Ask some of your colleagues to identify and document three ways AI is being utilized within your institution. Ask these colleagues to reflect on how these AI applications impact institutional operations and discuss your findings in team meetings.

CHAPTER 2
THE CRITICAL NEED FOR AN EVOLVING UNIFIED AI POLICY

It's very clear that AI is going to impact every industry. I think that every nation needs to make sure that AI is a part of their national strategy. Every country will be impacted.

—Jensen Huang, electrical engineer, co-founder, president, CEO of Nvidia

How Might We All Sing the Same Tune?

One of the major challenges I face is when teachers have different expectations of how students can or cannot use AI for their assignments. Some students have retorted that teacher A or B allows them to copy and paste the response or use AI as a credible source.

This is because the rate of AI integration for teachers is quite varied, and those who are more technologically inclined are running with it, while the others are either avoiding it or haven't had the time/support to explore it much.

It is often very clear when students have plagiarized their work using AI. So teachers have resorted to having follow-up conversations with students on the work submitted to help ascertain their learning. However, some teachers are more interested in "catching" students who have used AI than they are in teaching the students how to ethically use AI to support their learning. If the school adopted a unified approach to AI integration, many of these challenges could be mitigated.

—Experienced secondary teacher

In this chapter we will examine why a cohesive, institution-wide AI strategy is essential for success. A fragmented approach, where different departments or educators use AI tools in siloed or inconsistent ways, can lead to confusion, inequities, and missed opportunities. In contrast, a unified AI policy provides clear guidelines, supports professional development training and resources, and ensures that AI is leveraged in alignment with the institution's overall mission and values.

Co-creating an *evolving unified AI policy* (EUAIP) is crucial for several reasons, especially as AI technology is now prevalent in educational environments. Here are the key benefits of establishing such a policy:

1. Ensures Fair Use: A unified AI policy ensures that all students have equal opportunities to utilize AI tools. This helps prevent disparities in access and use, which can contribute to unequal learning outcomes.
2. Promotes Ethical Use: AI has potential misuses that may not be immediately apparent to students, such as recognizing biases. A well-defined policy establishes ethical boundaries and sets expectations for responsible use.
3. Protects Privacy: AI tools often process and store sensitive data. A unified AI policy helps safeguard student privacy and data security, outlining how data is collected, used, and protected.
4. Fosters Digital Literacy: By setting guidelines and expectations for AI use, a policy can also serve as an educational tool that teaches students about technology, including its capabilities, limitations, and implications.
5. Maintains Academic Integrity: An AI policy helps maintain the integrity of academic work. It clarifies what constitutes cheating and plagiarism in the context of AI, ensuring that students' work remains a true reflection of their own knowledge and abilities.
6. Manages Expectations: Both educators and students benefit from having clear expectations about how AI tools can and should be used in the learning process. This helps in consistently effectively integrating into the curriculum without undermining the educational goals.

7. Prepares for Future Challenges: As AI technology evolves, new challenges and scenarios will inevitably arise. A unified policy can provide a framework that can be adapted as circumstances change, ensuring ongoing relevance and effectiveness.

Why does a unified AI policy need to evolve? Helen Toner, an AI policy researcher and former board member of OpenAI, said in her Ted Talk in May 2024: "We need to focus on adaptability, not certainty." The rapid evolution of AI technologies necessitates a policy framework capable of responding to new developments and unforeseen challenges. An evolving AI policy ensures that regulations remain relevant and effective, fostering innovation while addressing ethical concerns, privacy issues, and potential risks.

By focusing on adaptability, policymakers can better accommodate the dynamic nature of AI advancements, creating a balanced approach that promotes both safety and progress. This flexibility is essential to navigating the complexities of AI, ensuring that a unified policy keeps pace with technological change and can be adjusted as our understanding of AI's impact deepens.

In summary, an EUAIP is essential for managing the integration of AI tools in educational settings in a way that supports ethical use, protects students, and enhances learning outcomes. It creates a structured yet dynamic set of principles where the benefits of AI can be maximized while minimizing potential risks and misunderstandings.

Designing an Evolving Unified AI Policy (EUAIP): A Six-Stage Process

Co-creating an EUAIP for use in schools can be efficiently structured as a six-stage process, drawing again from the principles of design thinking. This methodology ensures that the policy is not only comprehensive and practical but also closely aligned with the diverse needs of all stakeholders involved.

Design thinking is fundamentally user-centric, making it exceptionally suited for addressing complex issues like formulating an evolving unified AI policy in educational environments. By focusing on the specific needs and concerns of various groups, including students, teachers, administrators, and parents, this approach promotes thoroughness and inclusivity. It effectively addresses the critical elements of AI integration in schools, ensuring that the policy is both effective and equitable.

Figure 2.1:
The Design Thinking Stages

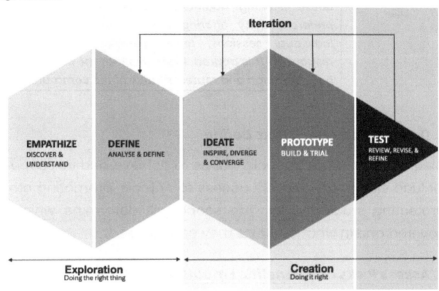

Designing for Learners' Agency:
The Design Thinking Framework

Iteration

EMPATHIZE	DEFINE	IDEATE	PROTOTYPE	TEST
DISCOVER & UNDERSTAND	ANALYSE & DEFINE	INSPIRE, DIVERGE & CONVERGE	BUILD & TRIAL	REVIEW, REVISE, & REFINE

Exploration
Doing the right thing

Creation
Doing it right

Adapted from Hasso-Plattner School of Design (d.school), Stanford University Marcus Lui and Dr Jennifer Chang Wathall

1. Engage Stakeholders: Empathize

Begin by involving and consulting all relevant stakeholders in the policy creation process. This group should include administrators, teachers, IT staff, students, parents, and possibly legal advisors, if deemed necessary. Engaging a diverse group ensures that the policy is comprehensive, addressing the needs and concerns of the entire school community. This stage aligns with the Empathize stage in the design thinking process, where we need to understand the needs, challenges, and emotions of those who will be impacted by our solutions. It requires deep listening and engagement to truly grasp the user experience from their perspective, ensuring that the outcomes are both relevant and beneficial. This approach will also foster buy-in and a sense of ownership over the unified AI policy once it is implemented.

Practical Tip: When conducting empathy interviews to gather diverse perspectives on AI use, start by developing a structured questionnaire that addresses key aspects such as ethical concerns, benefits, risks, and personal attitudes toward technology. Ensure comprehensive data collection by training interviewers in effective techniques, such as asking open-ended questions and employing active listening. Additionally, accommodate various respondent preferences by offering different interview formats, including individual sessions, focus groups, and anonymous written responses. This approach ensures that the information gathered is both thorough and representative of the community's views.

2. Define Goals and Scope: Define

Clearly define what the policy aims to achieve and its scope. Goals might include ensuring equitable access to AI tools, promoting ethical use, and protecting student data. The scope will determine which AI tools are covered and in what contexts they can be used.

3. Assess Risks and Benefits: Empathize and Ideate

Conduct a thorough assessment of the potential risks and benefits associated with AI use in the school setting. This assessment should consider privacy issues, potential for misuse, impact on learning, and ethical concerns. Understanding these factors will guide the development of a balanced and informed policy.

Here are some ways we can assess risks and benefits:

- **Review Current Literature and Case Studies:** Gather and analyze existing research, articles, and case studies about AI use in educational contexts. Look at both positive outcomes and challenges faced by other schools.
- **Survey Stakeholders:** Conduct surveys or focus groups with teachers, students, and parents to gather first-hand information about their expectations, concerns, and experiences with AI in education.

- **Identify Specific AI Applications:** List and evaluate the specific AI tools and technologies currently in use or being considered for use in the school.
- **Analyze Privacy Implications:** Examine how AI tools handle data privacy. Assess compliance with relevant laws and regulations, such as the Children's Online Privacy Protection Act (COPPA) or the General Data Protection Regulation (GDPR), depending on your location.
- **Evaluate Security Risks and Misuse Potential:** Assess the security measures of AI applications and the potential for misuse. Consider how AI might be used inappropriately by students or others and what safeguards are necessary to prevent such scenarios.
- **Consider Ethical Concerns:** Discuss the ethical implications of using AI, including issues related to fairness, bias, and accountability. Determine how these concerns can be addressed in the policy.
- **Develop Risk Management Strategies:** For each identified risk, develop strategies to mitigate it. This might include technical safeguards, user education, policy measures, and regular reviews of AI use.

4. Draft the Policy: Prototype

With the information gathered, draft the policy document. This should include guidelines on acceptable use, access rights, data privacy measures, ethical standards, and consequences for misuse, etc. It should also outline responsibilities for monitoring and enforcing the policy.

5. Review and Revise: Prototype and Test

Share the draft policy with all stakeholders for feedback. This review phase is crucial for identifying any oversights and ensuring the policy is clear and practical. Revise the policy based on this feedback, balancing the diverse needs and concerns of the school community. This aligns with the prototypes and testing stage in the design thinking process.

6. Implement and Educate

Once the policy is finalized, implement it across the school. This includes educating all stakeholders about their roles and responsibilities under the new AI policy. Professional development, informational materials, and ongoing support are key to successful implementation. Additionally, establish a mechanism for regularly reviewing and updating the policy to adapt to new technological developments or challenges.

By following these six stages, schools can develop an EUAIP that is thoughtful, comprehensive, and adaptable, ensuring that AI tools are used effectively and ethically to enhance educational outcomes.

Figure 2.2 outlines the six stages for designing an Evolving Unified AI Policy (EUAIP).

Figure 2.2:

Designing an Evolving Unified AI Policy (EUAIP)

DESIGNING AN EVOLVING UNIFIED AI POLICY

ENGAGE STAKEHOLDERS-EMPATHIZE

1 Involve key stakeholders such as administrators, teachers, IT staff, students, parents, and legal advisors in creating AI policies, ensuring their diverse needs and perspectives shape a comprehensive and embraced approach.

DEFINE GOALS & SCOPE- DEFINE

2 Clearly define what the policy aims to achieve and its scope. Goals might include ensuring equitable access to AI tools, promoting ethical use, and protecting student data.

ASSESS RISKS & BENEFITS-EMPATHIZE & IDEATE

3 Conduct a thorough assessment of the potential risks and benefits associated with AI use in the school setting.

DRAFT THE POLICY- PROTOTYPE

4 With the information gathered, draft the policy document.

REVIEW AND REVISE- PROTOTYPE AND TEST

5 Share the draft policy with all stakeholders for feedback. This review phase is crucial for identifying any oversights and ensuring the policy is clear and practical.

IMPLEMENT & EDUCATE

6 Implement the finalized AI policy school-wide, educating stakeholders on their roles with support and resources, and establish a routine for updates to adapt to technological changes and challenges.

An Example of a Unified AI Policy (EUAIP

Here is an example of a unified AI policy for student use that a school might create following the six-stage process outlined previously from GPT-4 from Poe.com retrieved May 2024:

Unified AI Policy (UAI) for Student Use

Anytown School District

Introduction

The Anytown School District recognizes the potential of artificial intelligence (AI) tools to enhance educational outcomes and support teaching and learning. This policy outlines the responsible use of AI technologies by students within the district to ensure ethical practices, protect privacy, and promote fairness.

Goals

1. To provide equitable access to AI resources.
2. To ensure that AI tools are used to support educational Goals.
3. To protect the privacy and security of student data.
4. To maintain academic integrity in the use of AI.

Scope

This policy applies to all AI-powered software and tools used in classrooms, for homework, and in any other school-related activities by students of Anytown School District.

Guidelines for Use

1. Access and Equity: All students will have equal access to AI tools approved by the district. No student will be disadvantaged by lack of access in their educational activities.

2. Ethical Use: Students must use AI tools in a manner that is honest and fair. Use of AI to complete assignments must always be disclosed.

3. Privacy and Security: Students must not use AI tools to store or transmit personal data without explicit permission from the school. The district will ensure all AI tools comply with applicable data protection laws.

---

4. Academic Integrity: Students are encouraged to use AI as a supplementary tool for learning. However, direct submission of 100% AI-generated work as their own is prohibited. Students must critically engage with and modify AI-generated content to reflect their understanding and cite the tools they used.

5. Monitoring and Enforcement: Teachers and school administrators will monitor the use of AI tools. Misuse will be addressed according to the school's academic integrity guidelines.

Implementation

1. Training: All students and staff will receive training on the ethical use of AI, including understanding this policy.

2. Awareness: Regular updates and reminders about the policy will be circulated through school newsletters and assemblies.

3. Support: IT support will be available to assist with the appropriate and effective use of AI tools.

Review

This policy will be reviewed annually by a committee comprising teachers, administrators, students, and parents to adapt to new developments in AI technology and education practices.

Adoption

Adopted by the Anytown School Board on [Date]

This example provides a framework that covers the core areas of concern, including access, ethical use, privacy, and academic integrity. It also emphasizes the ongoing process of training, support, and review to adapt to changing circumstances and technologies.

Synergy in Action:
Harmonizing AI and Human Input

Understanding AI use and its interplay with human input is crucial for developing a cohesive and effective AI policy. In the world of education, gauging the level of AI use is challenging due to its varied applications and the complex interaction between humans and AI. To illustrate this, I like to use the analogy of a chef and high-tech kitchen appliances. Imagine a busy modern kitchen where different appliances act as the ultimate sous-chefs. Precision

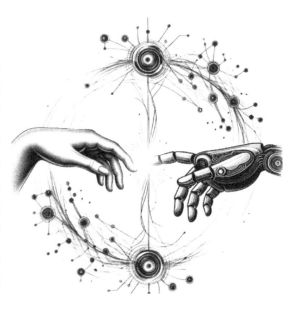

Image generated by DALL·E 3, 2024

tools like sous-vide machines meticulously maintain exact temperatures for perfect cooking, while advanced convection ovens ensure even and timely baking. My son loves using his sous-vide machine to slow cook a piece of fish for twelve to sixteen hours, allowing all the flavors to infuse perfectly. This tool allows him to achieve a level of precision that would be impossible with traditional cooking methods.

Similarly, in education, AI acts as a sophisticated toolset that enhances the capabilities of human educators. Just as a chef combines their unique touch with the precision of advanced appliances, educators can blend their pedagogical expertise with AI to create inquiry-based, engaging, and effective learning experiences. This coexistence emphasizes that the true potential of AI in education is realized not by replacing human elements but by working in harmony with them to achieve new heights of educational excellence.

Ultimately, it is the chef's decision, craft, and masterful use of techniques that produce the dish—just as a masterful teacher produces exceptional educational outcomes through the use of AI.

Figure 2.3 depicts how AI and human expertise can coexist harmoniously! There are two absolute boundaries rather than a scale. One end is marked "0%," where there's absolutely no AI being used—it's all human effort. The other extreme is marked "100%," where AI is used entirely without any human intervention, simply copying and pasting the output directly—a practice we aim to discourage.

You will notice that the space between these two extremes is shaded in gray, highlighting twenty examples of AI utilization that neither increase nor decrease in scale or intensity. This indicates that AI usage does not uniformly escalate from one end to the other. Instead, this gray area signifies a consistent blend of AI and human collaboration. Here, in this middle ground, the degree and intricacy of AI involvement is nuanced.

It's crucial to recognize that measuring the level of AI use, or quantifying it, poses significant challenges. The subject of AI utilization is inherently complex, influenced by a variety of factors that shape the interaction between AI and human efforts. This complexity suggests that the integration of AI doesn't follow a straightforward, linear path. Instead, it presents a complex interplay where the contributions of AI and human input vary widely, depending on the context and specific use case.

This model supports the idea that effective AI integration can occur at levels where AI tools consistently support pedagogical goals, such as enhancing interactive learning or streamlining administrative tasks, thereby fostering an environment where technology and human expertise coexist harmoniously to enhance educational outcomes.

Figure 2.3 illustrates a simple yet effective framework to conceptualize AI usage that reflects the nuances and complexity of the field; it is not a linear or progressive scale.

Figure 2.3:

Framework for Conceptualizing AI Usage

Harmonising AI and Human Input 100% AI Use

Brainstorm Ideas: Use AI to generate a list of topic ideas for essays or projects.

Re-craft Paragraphs: Improve the structure and flow of written paragraphs.

Summarize Texts: Quickly summarize long articles or chapters.

Assist Research: Find and compile relevant information on specific topics.

Create Study Guides: Generate study guides from provided course materials.

Translate Language: Translate texts or documents to understand or prepare multilingual materials.

Check Grammar and Spelling: Correct grammar and spelling in essays and reports.

Practice Pronunciation: Use language learning tools powered by AI to improve pronunciation.

Get Feedback on Writing Style: Use AI to receive feedback on writing style, tone, and clarity to improve essays and other written assignments.

Analyze Data: Analyze large sets of data for projects or research papers.

Generate Code: Use AI to assist in writing and debugging computer code.

Simulate Historical Event: Engage with AI-driven simulations to understand historical events better.

Simulate Experiments: Conduct virtual lab experiments with AI simulation tools.

Get Art and Design Inspiration: Generate art or graphic design ideas and prototypes.

Compose Music: Create or edit musical pieces with AI-assisted tools.

Predict Outcomes: Use AI to predict outcomes based on provided data, useful in subjects like economics or social sciences.

Enhance Presentations: Improve presentation quality with AI-driven design and content suggestions.

Experience Virtual Reality Learning: Explore virtual reality environments that are managed or enhanced by AI for immersive learning.

Automate Repetitive Tasks: Automate formatting, data entry, and other repetitive tasks to save time.

Organize Notes: Employ AI tools to help organize and categorize lecture notes, making study materials more accessible and easier to review.

0% AI Use

Chapter Summary

This chapter focused on the critical need for an evolving unified AI policy (EUAIP) within educational institutions. A fragmented approach to AI, where different departments or educators implement AI tools in siloed or inconsistent ways, can lead to confusion, inequities, and missed opportunities. In contrast, a cohesive, institution-wide AI strategy ensures that AI is used effectively, ethically, and equitably across the entire educational landscape.

The chapter outlined several key benefits of a unified AI policy:

1. Ensures Fair Use: Guarantees equal access to AI tools for all students, helping to prevent disparities that could affect learning outcomes.
2. Promotes Ethical Use: Establishes clear ethical boundaries and expectations for responsible AI use, including awareness of potential biases.
3. Protects Privacy: Details measures to safeguard sensitive data, addressing how student information is collected, used, and protected.
4. Fosters Digital Literacy: Acts as an educational tool that informs students about the capabilities, limitations, and implications of technology.
5. Maintains Academic Integrity: Defines standards regarding the use of AI in academic work to ensure that student outputs reflect their true capabilities.
6. Manages Expectations: Sets clear guidelines for how AI tools should be utilized in the educational process, aiding in their effective integration.
7. Prepares for Future Challenges: Provides a flexible framework that can evolve as new technologies and challenges emerge, ensuring the policy remains relevant.

The chapter also introduces a six-stage process for developing an evolving unified AI policy using design thinking principles:

1. Engage Stakeholders (Empathize): Involve all relevant parties in policy creation to ensure it meets the needs of the entire school community.
2. Define Goals and Scope (Define): Clearly articulate the aims and boundaries of the policy.
3. Assess Risks and Benefits (Empathize and Ideate): Evaluate the potential advantages and risks associated with AI use in education.
4. Draft the Policy (Prototype): Use the insights gathered to formulate the policy document.
5. Review and Revise (Prototype and Test): Solicit feedback to refine the policy, ensuring clarity and practicality.
6. Implement and Educate: Roll out the policy school-wide, providing necessary training and support.

An example of unified AI policy was provided to illustrate how these principles can be applied in practice. This example emphasized equitable access, ethical use, privacy protection, and academic integrity, all crucial for fostering a responsible AI-enhanced educational environment.

The chapter closed by acknowledging the complexity of determining AI usage levels in education, presenting a conceptual model that reflects the nuanced interplay between AI and human input. It introduced a conceptual model that captures the intricate relationship between AI and human input, illustrating how they can coexist in harmony. This model highlights the non-linear and multifaceted nature of AI integration, emphasizing that AI usage is most effective when it is strategically aligned with and enhances educational goals.

Discussion Questions

1. Assessing Impact: How could an evolving unified AI policy (EUAIP) specifically impact your teaching practices and the learning environment in your classroom? Discuss whether such a policy could alleviate any current challenges you face with AI technology.

2. Policy Development: Considering the six-stage process for developing an evolving unified AI policy introduced in the chapter, which stage do you think is most critical and why? How would you personally contribute to this stage in the policy development process at your institution?

3. Future Readiness: As AI technologies continue to evolve, how can an evolving unified AI policy remain adaptable to future challenges and technological advancements? Discuss strategies for keeping the policy relevant and effective over time.

Artefact opportunity

Draft a Mini AI Policy:

Collaboratively create a mini AI policy that you think your institution needs. Focus on key areas such as ethical AI use, data privacy, and academic integrity. Present your policy to the administration and discuss its potential impact on institutional practices.

CHAPTER 3
ETHICS AND
ACADEMIC INTEGRITY

To educate without ethics is to lead without a compass.
—GPT-4-128k, 2024

What Are the Ethical Considerations of Using AI in Education?

There is no denying the integration of AI into educational settings brings both transformative potential and significant ethical challenges. As with any powerful technology, it is essential to implement AI with careful consideration of these ethical implications to prevent harm and ensure alignment with the core educational values. Many organizations around the world have released their own AI ethics, principles, and guidance for education, including the following:

1. The United Nations Educational, Scientific, and Cultural Organization (UNESCO, 2021) developed ethical guidelines specifically for AI in education, stressing the importance of a humanistic approach to AI and education policies, aiming to protect human rights, foster skills for sustainable development, and promote effective human-machine collaboration. It advocates for AI to be human controlled

and focused on enhancing student and teacher capacities. The guidance also recommends exploring ways to balance open access with data privacy, ensuring ethical and transparent use of learner data. It calls for open discussions on AI ethics and data privacy, addressing potential negative impacts on human rights and gender equality. The guidelines also highlight the need for comprehensive regulatory frameworks to ensure ethical AI use, prioritizing data privacy and security for educators and students.

2. The Organisation for Economic Co-operation and Development (OECD, 2024) established AI Principles, which have been adopted by its member countries and include ethical guidelines relevant to the use of AI in education. The OECD recommendation on artificial intelligence outlines principles for the responsible use of trustworthy AI. Key ethical principles and recommendations include the following:

   a. **Inclusive Growth, Sustainable Development, and Well-Being:** Stakeholders are encouraged to use AI responsibly to foster benefits for society and the environment, including enhancing creativity, promoting inclusion, reducing inequalities, and protecting natural habitats.

   b. **Respect for the Rule of Law, Human Rights, and Democratic Values:** AI practitioners should maintain human rights, uphold democratic values, and ensure fairness across all stages of the AI system lifecycle, tackling issues like discrimination, privacy, data protection, and freedom of expression.

   c. **Transparency and Explainability:** Commitment to transparency is essential, requiring that AI systems be understandable and that their functionalities and limitations are clearly communicated.

   d. **Accountability:** AI actors must ensure the correct operation of AI systems and adhere to ethical standards, including traceable decision-making and systematic risk management.

3. The European Commission's High-Level Expert Group on AI has released the "Ethics Guidelines for Trustworthy AI," which covers ethical considerations for AI applications in various domains, including education. The guidelines emphasize three key components: legality, ethics, and robustness throughout the AI system's lifecycle. These guidelines stress the importance of adhering to ethical principles, respecting human autonomy, preventing harm, and ensuring fairness and explicability. They also highlight the need to address potential tensions between these principles, particularly in situations involving vulnerable groups or power imbalances. The document underscores the transformative and disruptive nature of AI technology, emphasizing the necessity of building AI systems that are worthy of trust to maximize benefits while mitigating risks and adverse impacts.

How Can We Address Ethical Challenges When Using AI?

Educators play a key role in shaping how AI tools are employed and understood within educational contexts. Therefore, it is essential we are equipped with the knowledge and tools necessary to promote responsible AI use, ensuring that these technologies serve as a complement to educational goals rather than a detriment.

The following points outline key areas of focus for institutions aiming to integrate ethical AI practices effectively:

- Explore the ethical considerations surrounding the use of AI in education, including issues of bias, privacy, and the impact on student agency.
- Provide practical guidance for the school community on how to promote responsible AI use in the classroom, including strategies for data privacy, algorithmic transparency, and critical evaluation of AI tools.

- Discuss the importance of teaching the entire school community about AI ethics and responsible digital citizenship.
- Offer resources and activities for educators to integrate AI ethics discussions into their curriculum.

Image generated by DALL·E 3 2024

Unethical Consequences of Uninformed AI Use

As AI technologies become increasingly integrated into educational environments, it is critical for institutions to be aware of the ethical challenges they pose. Figure 3.1 outlines examples of some of the ethical challenges of AI applications that all institutions need to be aware of.

Figure 3.1:

Unethical Consequences of Uninformed AI Use

UNETHICAL CONSEQUENCES OF UNINFORMED AI USE

INVASION OF PRIVACY

1 Indiscriminate gathering, storing, and analyzing of student data without proper consent and transparency can violate privacy rights. This includes unauthorized surveillance of student activities both online and in physical spaces.

BIAS AND DISCRIMINATION

2 AI systems can inherit or amplify biases present in their training data or algorithms, leading to discriminatory practices. This can manifest in biased admissions processes and unequal treatment of students based on race, gender, or socioeconomic status.

UUNDERMINING ACADEMIC INTEGRITY

3 AI tools can facilitate cheating and plagiarism if students use them to generate essays, solve homework without understanding, or carry out other assignments that are intended to be learning processes.

COMMERCIAL EXPLOITATION

4 There may be instances where educational institutions partner with AI vendors whose primary motive is profit rather than the educational welfare of students. This could lead to the prioritization of commercial interests over educational quality or student needs.

SECURITY RISKS

5 Insufficient security measures for AI systems can lead to data breaches and leaks of sensitive student information, putting students at risk of identity theft and other harm.

NEGLECTING ETHICAL TRAINING AND AWARENESS

6 Failing to educate and train students and educators on the ethical use of AI, including the potential risks and responsibilities associated with these technologies, can lead to misuse and negative repercussions.

Six-Step Ethical Decision-Making Process

By structuring ethical decision-making processes, institutions can ensure that their use of AI aligns with both their educational mission and ethical obligations, thereby fostering an environment of trust and integrity.

Institutions that integrate AI technologies face complex ethical decisions that require structured and transparent decision-making processes. The following gives some guidance about how these processes might be structured at the institutional level:

1. Form Ethical Committees or Boards

- Composition: These committees should be diverse, including members from various departments such as Technology, Academic Affairs, and Student Representation, and possibly external experts in ethics and technology. Alternatively, this could be a student-led committee fostering student agency.
- Role: The committee is responsible for guiding the ethical use of AI within the institution, making decisions on AI implementation, and addressing any ethical issues arising from its use.

2. Develop Ethical Framework and Principles

- Development: The committee should develop a set of ethical principles that will guide AI usage. These principles could include fairness, accountability, transparency, and respect for user privacy.
- Application: These principles serve as a benchmark for all AI-related decisions, ensuring that every action aligns with the institution's core values and ethical standards.

3. Involve Stakeholder Engagement

- Inclusion: Regular consultations with a broad range of stakeholders, including students, faculty, and administrative staff, ensure that diverse perspectives are considered.

- Feedback Mechanisms: Establishing channels through which stakeholders can voice concerns or suggestions about AI use helps maintain transparency and trust.

4. Use Ethical Impact Assessments (EIA)

- Procedure: Before any new AI tool is adopted, an ethical impact assessment (EIA) should be conducted. This assessment evaluates the potential ethical implications of the technology, considering factors like data privacy, potential biases, and the impact on student equity.
- Outcomes: The results of the EIA can lead to a go/no-go decision or might require modifications to the AI solution to align it with ethical standards.

5. Develop and Implement Policies

- Policy Crafting: Based on the ethical framework, develop specific policies governing AI use. These policies address issues such as data governance, user consent, and the transparency of AI processes.
- Implementation Strategies: Clear guidelines and procedures are established for implementing these policies, including training programs and communication plans.

6. Review and Update Regularly

- Monitoring: Continuous monitoring of AI technologies is essential to ensure they function as intended without ethical breaches.
- Policy Review: Ethical policies should be reviewed regularly to adapt to new challenges or advancements in AI technology. This could be annually or biennially, depending on the pace of technological change and experience within the institution.
- Adaptation: As AI technologies evolve, the ethical guidelines and policies may need to be updated. This iterative process ensures that the institution remains at the forefront of ethical AI use.

7. Report Regularly and Be Accountable

- Transparency: Regular reporting on AI use and its ethical implications enhances transparency. This could include an annual ethics report accessible to all stakeholders.
- Accountability: Clear mechanisms should be in place for holding individuals and departments accountable for breaches of ethical guidelines. This includes procedures for handling breaches and implementing corrective actions.

Further Guidance on Step 4: Ethical Impact Assessment (EIA)

One approach to evaluate the impact of a specific AI digital tool is to utilize an ethical impact assessment (EIA) framework, adapted from UNESCO (2023). It is crucial to customize the assessment questions to specifically address the implementation and effects of the AI tool within its designated environment. This ensures a focused evaluation that directly relates to the tool's usage and its potential consequences.

1. Purpose and Goals:

- What specific goals are intended to be achieved with this AI tool?
- In what specific contexts and by whom will this AI tool be used?

2. Stakeholder Engagement:

- Have you identified all stakeholders directly and indirectly affected by the deployment of this AI tool?
- What methods will be used to gather and incorporate feedback from these stakeholders into the ongoing development and refinement of the AI tool?

3. Ethical Principles:

- In what ways does the AI tool ensure adherence to ethical principles such as transparency, accountability, and fairness?
- How are potential biases in the data sets or algorithms identified and addressed?

4. Impact on Society:

- What are the anticipated positive contributions of the AI tool to society?
- Are there any foreseeable adverse effects on society, and how significant might these be?

5. Impact on Environment:

- What are the environmental implications of deploying this AI tool?
- What proactive measures are implemented to mitigate any negative environmental impacts?

6. Data Privacy and Security:

- What specific practices are in place to protect data privacy throughout the lifecycle of the AI tool?
- What are the security protocols to safeguard sensitive data against breaches?

7. Human Oversight and Control:

- What level of human oversight is integrated into the operation of the AI tool?
- How can users assert control over decisions made by the AI tool?

8. Mitigation Strategies:

- What specific actions are planned to mitigate any negative impacts identified?
- What mechanisms are in place to monitor and evaluate the effectiveness of these mitigation strategies?

9. Compliance and Accountability:

- How does the AI tool comply with applicable legal and regulatory standards?
- Who is responsible for addressing any ethical issues or negative outcomes that arise from the use of the AI tool?

10. Continuous Monitoring and Evaluation:

- What processes are established for ongoing monitoring and evaluation of the AI tool's ethical impact?

- How will the tool be updated or modified based on findings from continuous ethical reviews?

These questions are designed to provide a comprehensive overview of the ethical considerations associated with the deployment of a specific AI tool, ensuring that its use aligns with broader ethical standards and societal expectations.

Example of Six-Step Ethical Decision-Making Processes in Schools (Ideas from GPT-4-128k)

Elementary School: Student-Led Ethical AI Ethics Committee

Setting: Pine Grove Elementary School has introduced AI-powered learning tools in its classrooms. To ensure these tools are used ethically and promote inclusivity, the school established a student-led Ethical AI Committee.

Composition:

- The committee is primarily composed of students from grades 3 to 5, chosen based on their interest in technology and leadership qualities.
- It includes a faculty advisor (the technology teacher) and a parent liaison to provide guidance and ensure alignment with broader educational goals and ethical standards.

Role:

- The committee meets monthly to discuss how AI tools are being used in the classroom and any concerns or suggestions from their peers.
- They focus on ensuring that AI tools do not exclude any student, especially those with learning disabilities or limited access to technology at home.

Activities:

- Organize classroom visits to gather feedback on AI usage and understand different experiences and concerns.
- Host simple, student-friendly workshops explaining what AI is and how it should be used responsibly.
- Create posters and classroom presentations promoting ethical values related to AI, such as fairness and privacy.

Outcome:

- The committee presents a bi-annual report to the school board, summarizing their findings and recommendations, ensuring that the voice of the youngest stakeholders is heard in decisions about AI usage.

Teaching Students about Plagiarism and Proper Citation

In the quest to uphold academic integrity, some educators have resorted to AI detection tools as a deterrent against cheating and plagiarism, and we know this strategy just doesn't work. The variable reliability of these detection tools means that they often miss the mark, leading to a less effective crackdown on dishonest practices.

At the time of writing this book, AI detection systems are frequently hit or miss, failing to reliably identify all instances of academic dishonesty. Research conducted by Feizi and Huang (2023) at the University of Maryland revealed that current AI detectors result in "very high false-positive rates" and can be bypassed with simple techniques such as paraphrasing. The study highlighted that no AI detector currently available meets the necessary standards of accuracy and reliability for practical applications, such as identifying cheating.

Practical Tip – Avoid Relying on AI Detection Tools Due to Inaccuracy

AI detection tools, often used to identify plagiarism or cheating, can be inaccurate and lead to false positives or negatives. These tools may fail to recognize contextual nuances and are not always transparent in their analysis.

Further experiments by Weber-Wulff, Anohina-Naumec, Bjelobaba, et al. (2023)

indicated varying performance levels among AI detectors, leading to the conclusion that it's reasonable to expect that students can find ways to bypass any AI-detection tool, no matter how advanced it is.

Instead of solely depending on these fallible technologies, a more robust strategy would involve cultivating a strong ethical foundation in our students. By emphasizing the importance of academic integrity and honest conduct, we teach students not just to avoid cheating with AI, but also to navigate the complexities of an increasingly AI-driven future.

Teaching students about plagiarism is crucial in fostering academic integrity and respect for intellectual property. It involves explaining that plagiarism is the act of using someone else's work—whether from a book, article, or online source—without proper acknowledgment.

It's essential to emphasize the importance of citing all sources accurately, whether they are directly quoting, paraphrasing, or even using an idea that influenced their work. I also introduce them to various citation styles, like APA, MLA, or Chicago.

Referencing and Citing AI-Generated Material

Referencing and citing AI-generated content involves acknowledging that the content was produced by an AI system, which ensures transparency and maintains academic integrity. Here are some steps and considerations for properly citing AI-generated text:

1. Identify the AI Tool: Clearly state the name of the AI tool used to generate the text, such as "OpenAI's GPT-4-128," "Anthropic's Claude-3-Opus," etc.
2. Include the Date: Provide the date when the AI-generated content was created, as the outputs can vary over time due to updates or changes in the model.
3. Mention the Organization: If applicable, include the organization responsible for the AI tool, such as "Generated by OpenAI's GPT-4-128k, a tool developed by OpenAI."
4. Describe the Contribution: If the AI tool was used as part of a larger work, describe how it contributed. For example, "The initial draft was generated by Claude-3-Opus and was subsequently edited and verified by human authors."

5. Use a Standard Citation Format: Adapt the citation to fit within standard academic citation formats (APA, MLA, Chicago, etc.).

By following these guidelines, you can accurately and ethically cite AI-generated text in academic and professional contexts.

Here are examples of what the different citation methodologies may look like, retrieved from Purdue University https://guides.lib.purdue.edu/c.php?g=1371380&p=10135074:

APA

Guideline: https://apastyle.apa.org/blog/how-to-cite-chatgpt

Examples:

- APA format: OpenAI. (Year). ChatGPT (Month Day version) [Large language model]. https://chat.openai.com
- APA reference entry: OpenAI. (2023). ChatGPT (Feb 13 version) [Large language model]. https://chat.openai.com
- APA in-text citation: (OpenAI, 2023)

Example 1 from APA Guideline

When prompted with "Is the left brain right brain divide real or a metaphor?" the ChatGPT-generated text indicated that although the two brain hemispheres are somewhat specialized, "the notation that people can be characterized as 'left-brained' or 'right-brained' is considered to be an oversimplification and a popular myth" (OpenAI, 2023).

Reference
OpenAI. (2023). ChatGPT (Mar 14 version) [Large language model]. https://chat.openai.com/chat

MLA

Guideline: https://style.mla.org/citing-generative-ai/

Examples:

- MLA format: "Text of prompt" prompt. ChatGPT, Day Month version, OpenAI, Day Month Year, chat.openai.com.
- MLA Works Cited entry: "Explain antibiotics" prompt. ChatGPT, 13 Feb. version, OpenAI, 16 Feb. 2023, chat.openai.com.
- MLA in-text citation: ("Explain antibiotics")

Chicago

Recommendations on how to cite AI-generated content

Example:

Chicago style recommends citing ChatGPT in a Chicago footnote

Text generated by ChatGPT, March 31, 2023, OpenAI, https://chat.openai.com.

How to Mitigate Plagiarism

Plagiarism is a serious concern in academic and professional settings, undermining the integrity of work and the credibility of individuals. As educators and professionals, it is crucial to foster an environment that promotes originality and ethical practices. By implementing effective strategies, we can help students and colleagues understand the importance of producing authentic work and equip them with the tools to avoid plagiarism. Here are some practical tips to help mitigate plagiarism and encourage a culture of honesty and creativity.

Tip 1: Provide resources and support to ensure students have access to resources that help them understand how to use AI tools responsibly and cite sources correctly. Offer workshops or sessions on research skills and academic writing. Additionally, teaching proper citation techniques and the importance of giving credit where it's due can help cultivate a culture of academic integrity and respect for intellectual property.

Tip 2: Focus on the process of learning and creation rather than solely on the final product. Encourage students to engage deeply with their research topics, fostering a sense of ownership and personal connection to their work. Ask for drafts during lessons to allow close monitoring of student's development and provide targeted feedback. This proactive approach not only aids in spotting potential plagiarism but also supports students in honing their writing skills and reinforces the importance of academic honesty. This also allows you to monitor any abrupt changes in writing style or sudden improvements in the quality of content.

Tip 3: Understand your students and their unique communication styles. By forming a strong rapport and recognizing each student's distinct voice, we can better discern their authentic work.

Tip 4: Encourage critical analysis by assigning tasks that require students to apply their understanding in new and unique ways that AI tools cannot easily replicate. This could include personalized reflections, in-class presentations, or projects that require synthesizing information from multiple sources.

Tip 5: Use a viva voce to promote academic honesty. This oral examination method engages students directly, requiring them to articulate their understanding and defend their work in real time. Such face-to-face interaction not only reduces the opportunities for dishonest practices but also encourages a deeper grasp of the subject matter. By compelling students to explain their reasoning and thought processes, viva voce helps ensure the integrity of their academic achievements, fostering a culture of transparency and accountability in the educational process.

Tip 6: Promote academic integrity by fostering a culture of integrity and honesty within the classroom. Encourage students to take pride in their original work and see academic honesty as a valuable character trait. This can be reinforced through classroom discussions, integrity pledges, or integrating these values into the curriculum.

Tip 7: Clarify expectations and consequences at the beginning of the course and regularly thereafter. Clarify the rules regarding plagiarism and the use of digital tools based on a unified AI policy, which was discussed in the previous chapter. Make sure students understand what is considered acceptable and unacceptable behavior, including how and when AI tools can be used for their assignments.

Figure 3.2 summarizes these tips, providing a convenient reference that teachers can print out for easy access.

Figure 3.2:

Tips for Mitigating Plagiarism

HOW TO MITIGATE PLAGIARISM

RESOURCES & SUPPORT

1 Ensure students have access to resources that help them understand how to use AI tools responsibly and how to cite sources correctly.

FOCUS ON THE PROCESS: DRAFTS

2 Focus on the process of learning and creation rather than solely on the final product.Drafts during lessons to allow close monitoring of student's development and provide targeted feedback.

KNOW YOUR STUDENTS

3 Understand your students and their unique communication styles. Form a strong rapport and recognize each student's distinct voice to better discern their authentic work.

ENCOURAGE CRITICAL ANALYSIS

4 Assign tasks that require students to apply their understanding in new and unique ways that AI tools cannot easily replicate.

USE A VIVA VOCE

5 This oral examination method engages students directly, requiring them to articulate their understanding and defend their work in real-time

PROMOTE ACADEMIC INTEGRITY

6 Foster a culture of integrity and honesty within the classroom. Encourage students to take pride in their original work and to see academic honesty as a valuable character trait.

BE TRANSPARENT

7 Clarify expectations and consequences at the beginning of the course, and regularly thereafter, clarify the rules regarding plagiarism and the use of digital tools based on a unified AI policy

What to Do if You Suspect Plagiarism on a Draft

- Adopt Restorative Practices: Discuss approaches to handling instances of plagiarism that focus on learning and restoration rather than just punishment. Include methods for helping students learn from their mistakes and understand the importance of academic honesty.
- Conduct a One-to-One Discussion with the Student: Arrange a private meeting with the student to discuss the issue. Present your findings clearly and calmly. Ask the student to explain how they compiled their work and listen to their side of the story. This can be an educational moment rather than purely punitive. If you suspect plagiarism or improper use of AI, engage the student in a reflective dialogue. Ask them to discuss the thought process behind their work and how they used external tools. This can help them understand their missteps and learn from them.
- Offer Second Chances: When appropriate, allow students to revise their plagiarized draft work after discussing the issue. This approach emphasizes learning and improvement over punishment, helping students recognize and correct their mistakes.
- Provide Constructive Feedback: Offer guidance on how the student can rectify the situation. This might involve rewriting the paper, providing the correct citations, or completing an additional assignment on plagiarism and citation. The goal is to educate them on why plagiarism is harmful and how they can avoid it in the future.

Practical Tip: Never let it get to the stage of plagiarism on a final assignment if you can help it!

Always address plagiarism prevention early on to avoid issues with final assignments. Implement clear guidelines and provide resources on proper citation and ethical research practices from the start, ensuring students understand and adhere to academic integrity standards throughout their work.

Chapter Summary

Chapter 3 discussed the ethical considerations necessary when integrating AI in educational settings, emphasizing both the potential benefits and inherent risks. It highlighted the critical role of educators in ensuring that AI technologies are implemented responsibly to support educational goals without compromising ethical standards.

Key Ethical Challenges:

The chapter outlined several ethical challenges associated with AI in education, including the following:

- **Privacy Concerns:** Issues arise from the potential for invasive data collection practices without proper consent.
- **Bias and Discrimination:** AI systems may perpetuate existing biases, leading to unfair treatment of students.
- **Academic Integrity:** There's a risk of AI tools being used for cheating and plagiarism.
- **Commercial Exploitation:** Partnerships with AI vendors might prioritize profit over educational quality.
- **Security Risks:** Weak security in AI systems can lead to data breaches.
- **Lack of Ethical Training:** Insufficient emphasis on teaching the ethical use of AI can lead to misuse.

Ethical Decision-Making Framework:

To address these challenges, the chapter recommends establishing robust ethical frameworks within educational institutions, including the following:

- **Ethical Committees:** Forming diverse committees to oversee AI implementation and address ethical issues.
- **Stakeholder Engagement:** Involving a broad spectrum of stakeholders to ensure diverse perspectives in AI-related decisions.

- **Ethical Impact Assessments (EIA):** Conducting assessments to evaluate the ethical implications of new AI tools.
- **Policy Development:** Crafting and implementing policies based on established ethical principles.
- **Regular Review and Adaptation:** Continuously monitoring and updating policies to adapt to new challenges and advancements in AI.
- **Reporting and Accountability:** Ensuring transparency and accountability in AI usage through regular reporting and clear mechanisms for addressing ethical breaches.

Practical Guidance for Educators:

Educators are provided with practical advice on promoting responsible AI use:

- **Integrating AI Ethics into Curriculum:** Suggestions include teaching students about AI ethics and responsible digital citizenship.
- **Mitigating Academic Dishonesty:** Strategies to combat plagiarism and cheating, such as promoting a culture of academic integrity and using tools like viva voce examinations to authenticate student knowledge.

Discussion Questions

1. Defining Ethical Boundaries: How do you define ethical boundaries for using AI in your own educational setting? Discuss the potential ethical dilemmas you might face with AI integration and how these can be addressed according to the principles outlined in the chapter.

2. Role of Ethical Committees: If your school were to establish an Ethical Committee to oversee the use of AI, what roles and responsibilities would you assign to it? Who should be included in this committee to ensure a diverse and comprehensive representation of stakeholders?

3. Promoting Academic Integrity: Discuss strategies that could effectively reduce the instances of cheating and plagiarism facilitated by AI tools. How can educators foster a deeper understanding and commitment to academic integrity among students in an environment increasingly dominated by digital tools?

Artefact Opportunity

Ethical Review Panel:

Form an ethical review panel comprising colleagues from different departments. Task the panel with evaluating a current or proposed AI application within the institution. The panel should assess the ethical implications, potential biases, and privacy concerns associated with the AI tool. After the review, present the findings and recommendations to the larger school community for discussion and action.

PART 2

EDUCATOR ENGAGEMENT: EMPOWERING TEACHERS

HOW CAN WE AMPLIFY TEACHER AGENCY THROUGH EFFECTIVE AI INTEGRATION, SAVING TIME AND STREAMLINING WORKFLOW?

Image generated by DALL·E 3, 2024

CHAPTER 4

MAPPING THE JOURNEY:
UNDERSTANDING THE STAGES IN AI ADOPTION

All great achievements require time.
—Maya Angelou, American memoirist, poet, and civil rights activist

Where Am I in My Journey of AI Integration?

Hansei: The Art of Self-Reflection and Growth

In the pursuit of personal and professional growth, the concept of *hansei*—a Japanese term for self-reflection—plays an essential role. Hansei is more than just a momentary pause to think about one's actions; it is a deeply ingrained cultural practice that involves acknowledging mistakes, understanding their impact, and taking actionable steps to improve.

The importance of hansei lies in its power to foster continuous improvement. By regularly engaging in self-reflection, individuals can identify areas where they have fallen short and develop strategies to address these shortcomings. This process not only enhances personal accountability but also encourages a mindset of lifelong learning.

In educational settings, hansei can be a transformative tool for both educators and students. Educators who practice self-reflection can better understand their teaching methods, recognize what works well and what doesn't, and adapt their strategies to meet the needs of their students more effectively. For students, hansei promotes critical thinking and self-awareness, helping them take ownership of their learning journey and develop resilience in the face of challenges.

Image generated by DALL·E 3, 2024.

Metacognition and self-reflection are critical components in learning. By understanding one's own thinking processes and position in the learning journey, individuals can effectively navigate the complexities of AI integration. This self-awareness enables us to recognize our current competencies and limitations, allowing us to identify specific areas where additional knowledge or skills are required.

With this insight, educators can tailor their learning paths to better harness AI's potential, addressing gaps and leveraging strengths. Ultimately, fostering metacognition empowers learners to make informed decisions and take meaningful steps forward in integrating AI into their practices.

The journey of AI-powered pedagogy adoption can be effectively understood through a four-stage framework: Survive, Strive, Thrive, and Arrive, as seen in figure 4.1. This structured framework provides a powerful tool for self-reflection and professional growth, enabling educators and institutions to assess their current utilization of AI technologies and strategically plan their progression through the stages.

Each stage represents a different level of proficiency and AI use—from initially grappling with basic implementation (Survive), to actively learning and refining its use (Strive and Thrive), and, ultimately, transforming curriculum and instruction (Arrive).

A few years ago, I was collaborating with educators at an international school that had just hired a new head. One evening over dinner, he confided in me that he felt completely overwhelmed and inadequate, constantly firefighting and stuck in survival mode since he arrived. I noticed that he was constantly rushing from meeting to meeting and always highly stressed and flustered! Even during dinner, he was constantly on his phone, checking for messages. And this was post-Covid! He genuinely believed he wasn't doing a great job. I shared the four-stage model for integrating new systems: starting with the firefighting mode—Survive—and then moving to Strive, Thrive, and Arrive.

As he looked at the graphic, I could see a wave of relief wash over his face. The model reassured him that starting in survival mode is a natural part of most journeys. Realizing that progressing through these stages was normal, especially as the head of a new school, he felt more confident and motivated. Embracing each phase, he understood that gradual improvement would lead to significant educational transformation.

As you embark on integrating AI into your teaching practices, understanding these stages becomes crucial. By reflecting on where you currently stand in the adoption of AI technologies and envisioning where you aim to go, you equip yourself to make more informed decisions and adapt more effectively to changes. This self-awareness is key not only to leveraging new technologies but also to enhancing your pedagogical strategies in a way that meets the evolving needs of your students. Let's explore how each stage of AI adoption can help refine your approach and transform your educational environment.

The Stages of AI-Powered Pedagogy Adoption

Integrating any technology into education is more like a journey with multiple cyclical stages. As educators and schools start using new digital tools, including AI, they often find themselves moving through four key stages. But here's the interesting part: these stages aren't a straight line. Instead, they loop around in a cycle, reflecting how the needs in education and the capabilities of technology keep evolving. This means schools and individuals can move back and forth between stages as they figure out what works best. This cyclical pattern is really about staying adaptable and making sure that as technology changes, the way we teach can change with it. So as we dive into these four stages of adopting AI tools in education, think of it as mapping out a flexible, iterative path to enhancing learning with AI technology.

Figure 4.1 illustrates the four stages of AI adoption.

Figure 4.1:
The Stages of AI Adoption

The Firefighting Stage!

Trying to choose which AI tools to use. Provide information to school community e.g., teachers, parents, students.

Teacher Adoption & Play Time!

Teachers given time to learn how to use different AI tools Establish academic integrity and Ethics Protocols

What AI digitals tools do we use? Which AI tools are useful for teachers and students?

How do the AI digital tools work? What guidance do teachers/students need? What PD do teachers need on the tools?

Survive **1** **Strive**

4 **AI ADOPTION** **2**

Arrive **3** **Thrive**

Total Transformation of Pedagogy

Utilizing AI to create new pedagogies that were previously unimageable.

Enhancing Learning Through Pedagogy

Offering professional development sessions Incorporating AI to enhance learning

How do we redesign an entire unit utilizing AI which involves the best pedagogical practices and previously inconceivable ideas?

What PD do teachers need that focuses on effective pedagogy and learning? How to use the AI digitals tools in a meaningful way to enhance learning?

Please note it is normal and expected for teachers to cycle back to earlier stages, such as the Survive stage, whenever new tools are introduced or existing tools evolve. This cyclical process supports ongoing adaptation and mastery over time. Each loop through the stages enables a deeper understanding, more refined skills, and greater integration of AI into pedagogical practices, contributing to continuous professional growth and educational innovation. This approach ensures that educators remain agile and responsive to the changing landscape of technology in education.

The first stage, Survive, is about evaluating and choosing AI digital tools that align with educational goals. It also involves keeping teachers, parents, and students informed with updates and key information to prepare them for new technological integrations.

The second stage is Strive, where the focus is on teacher adoption and playtime. In this stage, there needs to be dedicated time for teachers to explore and master digital tools, enhancing their comfort and proficiency. This stage includes establishing a strong foundation in digital citizenship for responsible and ethical online interactions, as well as developing and enforcing protocols to maintain academic integrity and proper netiquette.

The third stage is Thrive, which involves using AI tools to enhance learning through pedagogy. In this stage, professional learning sessions are provided and focused on integrating AI tools into innovative teaching practices. This stage aims to implement AI in ways that significantly improve the learning experience, ensuring technology effectively supports educational goals.

The fourth (and not necessarily final) stage in the framework, Arrive, facilitates the systematic adoption of AI while also aligning its use with the overarching goals of educational institutions, ultimately fostering a more effective and innovative learning environment. Through this progression, educators undergo significant professional development, equipping them with the necessary skills to navigate and capitalize on the evolving landscape of educational technology.

The arrows on this graphic emphasize the dynamic and evolving nature of technology adoption in education, allowing for flexibility and continuous development as educators navigate through these stages repeatedly.

Practical Tip: AI-Powered Pedagogy Adoption Stages are Cyclical Stages and Iterative

Remember, the stages of AI adoption—Survive, Strive, Thrive, and Arrive—are not linear but cyclical and iterative. It's completely normal to revisit earlier stages as new technologies emerge or as your teaching context changes. Embrace this flexibility as a natural part of growth and adaptation in educational technology. This iterative process allows you to continuously refine and enhance your use of AI, ensuring that your teaching strategies remain effective and responsive to both technological advancements and educational needs.

Figure 4.2 provides a summary of each of the four stages in AI-powered pedagogy adoption that you can print off for easy reference and use as a visual guide during planning sessions or professional development workshops.

Figure 4.2:

Printable version of Four Stages of AI-Powered Pedagogy Adoption

The Four Stages of AI-Powered Pedagogy Adoption

1. Survive: The Firefighting Stage

Key Steps:

- Tool Selection: Evaluate and select AI digital tools that are well-suited to meeting educational goals.
- Community Engagement: Actively provide updates and important information to all members of the school community, including teachers, parents, and students, to prepare them for new technological integrations.

2. Strive: Teacher Adoption & Playtime

Key Steps:

- Hands-on Learning: Allocate dedicated time for teachers to explore and become proficient with various digital tools, enhancing their comfort and competence.
- Digital Citizenship Setup: Build a strong foundation in digital citizenship to ensure responsible and ethical online interactions.
- Integrity and Ethics Protocols: Create and enforce protocols focused on maintaining academic integrity and proper netiquette.

3. Thrive: Enhancing Learning Through Pedagogy

Key Steps:

- Professional Development: Offer professional development sessions that focus on integrating AI tools into innovative pedagogical practices.
- Pedagogical Enhancement: Implement AI in ways that support and significantly improve the learning experience, ensuring that technology serves educational goals effectively.

4. Arrive: Total Transformation of Pedagogy

Key Steps:

- Innovative Integration: Adopt AI tools to explore and establish new pedagogical methods that were previously unimaginable, thereby transforming educational practices.
- Continual Evolution: Promote a culture of ongoing learning and adaptation, where AI tools are consistently reassessed and refined to align with the evolving educational landscape.

All images were generated using
DALL·E 3, 2024

Educators and institutions may find themselves revisiting these stages multiple times as they adapt to new technologies, learn from experiences, and continuously strive to improve and transform educational practices with AI. This cyclical model supports a flexible and adaptive approach to technology adoption in education.

Figure 4.3 is a self-reflection tool for you to use to track which state you are in at any particular time.

Figure 4.3:

Self-Reflection Tool for AI Adoption

Self-Reflection Tool for Teachers:
The Four Stages of AI-Powered Pedagogy Adoption

1. Survive: The Firefighting Stage

What AI digitals tools do we use?

Which AI tools are useful for teachers and students?

Which tools are we going to subscribe to as a school?

2. Strive: Teacher Adoption & Playtime

How do the AI digital tools work?

What guidance do teachers/students need?

What Professional Development do teachers need on the tools?

3. Thrive: Enhancing Learning Through Pedagogy

What Professional Development do teachers need that focuses on effective pedagogy and learning?

How to use the AI digitals tools in a meaningful way to enhance learning?

4. Arrive: Total Transformation of Pedagogy

How do we redesign an entire unit utilizing AI which involves the best pedagogical practices and previously inconceivable ideas?

All images were generated using DALL·E 3, 2024

The stage I am at currently is _ _ _ _ _ _ _ _ _ _ _ because _ _ _ _ _ _ _ _ _ _ _ _.
The next stage is _ _ _ _ _ _ _ _ _ _ as I need to _ _ _ _ _ _ _ _ _ _ _

The four stages of AI-powered pedagogy—Survive, Strive, Thrive, and Arrive—offer a robust framework that can effectively guide any e-learning adoption. Each stage addresses a specific phase of integration, from initial adaptation to full-scale utilization of AI tools in educational settings. For instance, during the Covid-19 pandemic, an international school successfully adopted this model to transition to remote learning. This case study exemplifies how the model helps institutions systematically adopt any kind of educational technology to excel in the new digital teaching landscape.

Here is a case study from Sandra Chow, describing how she used a four-stage framework with her leadership team during Covid:

The Stages of e-Learning has been a very helpful framework for our school throughout Covid-19. At our school, the pandemic hit us right after the Chinese New Year break in February 2020, and our school, like many others, was not readily prepared for what was to come. We had to literally build the plane while it was flying. But we had a fantastic team of leaders, teachers, and staff who took on the challenge as we took flight. Right about this time, when we were preparing distance learning plans; outlining our training strategy to upskill our teachers; coordinating with government officials, education bureaus, and fellow educators facing the same challenge; and making sure our systems were up to speed, Dr. Jennifer Chang Wathall posted the Stages of e-Learning framework on social media.

As a leadership team, we immediately felt that this framework helped to make sense of all the emotions and tension that were building up, while also giving us a direction to strategize and plan. It provided a common language for everyone to express their feelings and know that their feelings were "normal." In addition, the framework provided a pathway toward hope and stability.

During one of our early training sessions, we introduced the framework to staff and did a Mentimeter poll in order to gain insight into where the staff felt like they were at. This helped us as a digital and innovative learning team to know what kind of training and support was needed at that time. The graphic on the right represents the type of training our team focused on

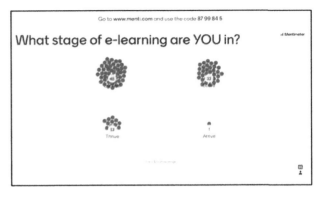

depending on the stages we determined the teachers were at.

During the **Survive** stage of e-learning, teachers needed basic support of core systems. The phrase "Maslow before Bloom" was a very common phrase used by ed tech leaders because when it came to the type of training that teachers needed at this stage, it had to be basic. Teachers are often overwhelmed by the systems they need to get online and connect with their students. So at this stage, our team focused on Microsoft Teams (our video conference platform), Seesaw (used by our primary school), and tools to help teachers create videos for asynchronous learning. Asynchronous learning was another decision made early on in our Survive stage, because it allowed for more time to equip our teachers and students. Teaching asynchronously was much less complicated and allowed for more breathing time to get familiar with distance learning.

As teachers slowly moved from the **Survive** to the **Strive** stage and were more ready for additional learning, we began introducing more varieties of digital tools that would be helpful in the classroom. This included assessment tools, tools to bring interactivity in synchronous settings, and the more advanced features of our core systems. Likewise, we also started bringing in best practices and strategies for online/remote learning that would help make interactions more dynamic and the learning process more effective.

At the **Thrive** and **Arrive** stages, teachers were fully ready to embrace ideas that would help improve their feedback to students and to explore different assessment strategies. As a leadership team and for our coaches, the framework really helped us to keep a pulse on how to better support our learning community and help us all improve our practice.

The other thing we noticed as 2020 progressed was that as our teachers fell into stride and more people moved into the **Thrive** or **Arrive** stage, Covid-19 kept us nimble. As soon as distance learning got

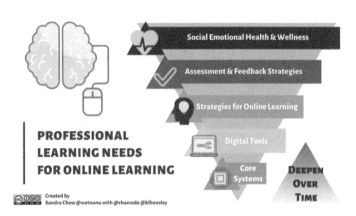

comfortable, a new twist would be introduced and we would have to begin hybrid teaching or go back to distance learning. This was the case when school started again in August 2020. Even though teachers and students already had experience with distance learning from the previous school year, starting a brand-new school year with new students, parents, and teachers meant that we quickly shifted back to the **Survive** or **Strive** stage again.

We've always known that as educators, like students, we should be lifelong learners, but Covid-19 really kept us on our toes. The e-Learning Stages, or dare I say "Learning Stages," continues to be a framework that helps our school community remember that we're not always going to be perfect teachers who have mastered every aspect of teaching.

We are constantly learning, and there may be times when we are in the **Survive** or **Thrive** stage, and that is okay. This might occur when we start teaching at a new school, after returning to school after a maternity or long-term sick leave, or when we switch grades, subjects, or courses. The important thing to remember is that **Thriving** or **Arriving** is just around the corner, and it just takes time.

Thank you to Jennifer for making this process visual for us! 😊

Sandra Chow

K–12 Educator and Leader

Here is another case study from an organization that used this four-stage model during Covid:

This graphic by Dr. Jennifer Chang Wathall represents an apt description of the practical and emotional stages of learning. As we have all needed to adapt to e-learning and the reality of what that entails in our school contexts, words such as **"strive," "survive," "arrive,"** and **"thrive"** resonate with the journey we have been on . . . moving from being almost passengers and observers to drivers and active participants. What e-learning looks like, sounds like, and feels like during each of these stages is very different and unique to the stage that schools, teachers, learners, and parents are at. The framework provided us with a common language that effectively connected our schools across cities, countries, and continents during the pandemic.

For me, the Survive stage was all about logistics, communication, and monitoring the well-being of our learning community—leaders, teachers, support staff, students, and parents. Answering the who, what, where, when, why, and how questions was paramount. Individual roles as a learner, parent, and teacher had now been dramatically altered. The technological readiness required for this at all levels provided an opportunity for a steep learning curve for everyone to take part in.

The Strive stage was the finding out of how these technological tools actually work. How can they be used and adapted to suit the current reality we are in? Who can support me so that I feel confident and secure in making learning happen for my students?

Thrive was all about being able to take a breath and have a moment to reflect on the impact thus far, monitoring levels of effectiveness from a 360-degree perspective and making the changes to ensure improved provision. This provided an opportunity for educators to be creative and take some risks with the teaching which they may not have had the opportunity to in a face-to-face, brick-and-mortar school setting.

Arrive was all about feeling like we had managed to reach a point where most of us—leaders, teachers, students, and parents—were comfortable and happy with the online learning provision on offer, the uptake and participation levels of students engaged in the online learning model, and the quality of the teaching and learning that were taking place.

As I reflect on this journey, what has worked well and what has not, some general guidelines come to mind if we were to ever have to undergo this process again. The following are my top tips:

1. Less is more. Quality over quantity. Adapt the school day, condense the timetable, and include blended learning of synchronous and asynchronous learning. Provide flexibility for students to be able to complete tasks in their own time (asynchronous) as well as having some live sessions in which they interact with the teacher and their peers (synchronous).
2. Balance time on screen. Then initial input, mid-lesson checkpoint, and end-of-lesson plenary are live; however, students continue with the learning offline. Teachers are available for queries and clarification throughout the day using chat functions on the digital platform used.

3. Vary class interactions. Do lessons as a whole class, in small groups, or 1:1. Allow time for students to engage in collaborative groups, and build that into a weekly and daily schedule.
4. Personalization and connectivity are key. This is an opportunity to build on the student-teacher as well as parent-teacher rapport and relationship. Understanding each family's context of reality is important to providing empathy and flexibility so all students and families access the learning.
5. Monitor student and teacher connections carefully. Where students are less engaged, we phone home and make alternative arrangements.
6. It is important to make good use of teaching assistants where available—they are a precious resource!
7. It is important to provide meaningful feedback to students on their work. Give flexibility to students on how they upload their work.
8. Continue with such events as whole-school assemblies, special events online, fitness and well-being activities that promote team spirit, and positivity to ensure a sense of belonging for students, parents, and teachers.
9. It is not just "academic" learning that is the focus. Social interaction and learning are important as well as we continue to communicate what fun learning is and what that looks like—whether it is in the real or online environment.
10. Events on the school calendar continue to be celebrated. WWF summits, the PYP Exhibition, and World Book Day still take place—just adapted to an online platform.

As we receive news from governments that schools are introducing a phased return to learning in a brick-and-mortar setting, we revert back to the original graphic and the stage of Survival. What do we need to put in place in order to survive this new challenge?

Continuing the Conversation

How can this graphic for learning be used within your own professional learning context?

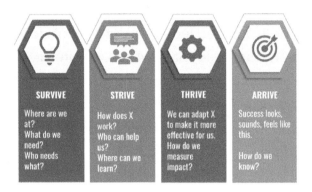

Initially, it was used during school closures to identify what stage we were at with coping with online learning and the new landscape of what teaching and learning looked like for us on different levels—as individuals, as departments, as schools, and as an organization.

I also used it as a well-being check-in point with our leaders and heads of schools. The graphic was pivotal in calming us down and provided us with big-picture moments. In the midst of the panic of school closures, it was easy to just try to go quickly from A to B—and feel bad and guilty when outcomes did not reach expectations. This gave us a calm approach to simply say, "This is where we are at now. It is not saying we will always stay here, but for now, that is where we are, and we need to be in this stage until we feel physically, emotionally, and logistically comfortable to move on." Being able to provide a strategic plan was very useful. Giving concrete action points to our journey ahead was crucial. This really helped give leaders and teachers an approach and common language to use when speaking with parents and students. It saved us from running around like headless chickens, trying to get things done but not really accomplishing anything. I recall seeing that graphic when I was introduced to it, and it was an aha moment for me.

We also gave our leaders and heads of school the opportunity to identify the stage they were at and "tell us more." It was an opportunity to identify the next steps that would need to be accomplished in order to feel comfortable at the next stage. What does Arrive look like, sound like, feel like?

I used it as a success criteria and checklist for us to track the journey of how we can get from here to there. As we returned to face-to-face and hybrid/blended learning, our schools faced new challenges. And so, we use the model to identify where we are at, why we think we are at that stage, what success and thriving looks like, and our action points—individually and/or collectively—to get to that point. It is used as an opportunity for schools to celebrate their authentic journey—the successes as well as the pitfalls.

Moving forward, I am working with schools on school development. So I now use it so that as schools identify an area/initiative they would like to roll out or see a need for, we use those terms and create a concise picture of what each stage looks like for us.

Survive - What do we use now? What is the current state of play?

Strive – What tool/process/protocol do we want to use? How does X work?

Arrive – What does success look like?

Thrive – How can we challenge ourselves further? What are our next steps?

And the cycle continues. I have encouraged schools to also use it with students as a way for them to develop their own "action plan."

Oanh Crouch, director of education at Globeducate.

Website: www.globeducate.com

Globeducate is an organization of schools across Europe, UK, Africa, North America, and Asia.

Chapter Summary

This chapter explored a structured pathway for integrating AI-powered pedagogy into educational practices through metacognition and self-reflection. It emphasized the importance of educators understanding their learning processes and their current stage in the AI integration journey. By identifying their competencies and limitations, educators can pinpoint areas needing further development, tailoring learning paths to maximize the potential of AI tools in education.

The chapter introduced a four-stage framework for AI-powered pedagogy adoption: Survive, Strive, Thrive, and Arrive. These stages represent different levels of proficiency and integration, from tackling initial challenges to mastering AI integration to transform educational practices. The stages are cyclical and iterative, reflecting the ongoing nature of technological adaptation.

A couple of case studies using this four-stage model were discussed. These case studies involved international organizations who use the model during the Covid-19 pandemic. One school progressed from urgent digital tool adoption (Survive) to enhancing online teaching capabilities (Strive and Thrive) and ultimately refining their AI and digital application (Arrive), while another organization used the model to address their varying professional learning needs.

Discussion Questions

1. Reflection on Personal Experience: Reflecting on your own experiences, which stage of AI-powered pedagogy adoption do you currently find yourself in? Discuss any challenges you have faced during this stage and how you have addressed them.

2. Cyclical Nature of Learning: How does the cyclical and iterative nature of the four-stage framework affect your perception of progress and success in integrating AI into your teaching practices? Share examples of situations where you might have moved back a stage and how that impacted your overall strategy.

3. Survive to Strive Transition: Transitioning from the Survive to the Strive stage involves a shift from tackling initial challenges to actively engaging with AI tools. Can you discuss a particular instance or strategy that helped you make this transition effectively in your educational setting?

4. Maximizing AI Tools: Considering your current use of AI tools, what specific competencies do you think you need to develop further to move from Thrive to Arrive? How do you plan to acquire these competencies?

5. Self-Reflection Tool Utilization: How effective do you find the self-reflection tool (figure 4.3) provided in the chapter for assessing your stage in the AI adoption process? Discuss how this tool has or hasn't helped you in planning your professional development or adapting your teaching strategies.

Artefact Opportunity

Self-Assessment of AI Integration:

Self-assess your current stage in AI adoption (Survive, Strive, Thrive, or Arrive). Identify specific actions you can take to progress to the next stage and share your plans in departmental meetings.

CHAPTER 5

HARMONIZING AI PRINCIPLES WITH PEDAGOGICAL PRINCIPLES

The whole art of teaching is only the art of awakening the natural curiosity
of young minds for the purpose of satisfying it afterwards.
—Anatole France, French poet, journalist, and novelist

How Can AI Facilitate a Pedagogical Paradigm Shift from Traditional, Teacher-Centered Models to a More Student-Centered, Inquiry-Based Approach?

Since OpenAI made ChatGPT available, I have been enthusiastically exploring GenAI, which has significantly enhanced my productivity and efficiency. I take advantage of GenAI as a thinking partner to troubleshoot problems, brainstorm solutions, and explore various scenarios before initiating projects. For example, before launching the Student Entrepreneur Project, I used ChatGPT to create lesson plans and identify logistical challenges.

To support student learning, I created a chatbot using Magic School to facilitate feedback on design projects. I explored how GenAI could help generate feedback and ideas with my Year 7 (Grade 6) students. We discussed the importance of verifying the accuracy of responses and maintaining personal data privacy. When using GenAI with students, teachers must be aware of age limitations so that the generated content is appropriate, both in terms of complexity and subject matter and in compliance with privacy regulations. I wrote specific prompts for the chatbot available in Magic School and modeled how to seek feedback. This controlled environment not only ensures quality output from GenAI but also guides students on effective question formulation and input entry.

I have benefited greatly from integrating GenAI into my work as a teacher and curriculum coordinator. We have heard a lot, "GenAI is here to stay." As educators, we need to develop agility in learning how to utilize GenAI productively, responsibly, and ethically. This requires a proactive approach to understanding GenAI capabilities and limitations, and how to integrate them effectively into teaching and learning practices."

Alison Ya-Wen Yang
International Educator and Leader

This chapter explores the transformative potential of AI in reshaping educational landscapes. As educational paradigms shift from traditional, teacher-centered models to more student-centered, inquiry-based approaches, AI emerges as a pivotal vehicle to support this. This chapter delves into how AI can be harmonized with pedagogical strategies to

Image generated by DALL·E 3, 2024

enhance educational outcomes. It is crucial to move beyond purely adopting AI technology that reinforces what teachers have always done; educators must intertwine AI with solid pedagogical foundations to foster student engagement, promote critical thinking, and accommodate diverse learning needs.

We discuss how harmonizing AI principles with effective pedagogical tenets can impact the planning of learning experiences and the design of units of inquiry. This integration promises to not only uphold the ethical and effective use of AI in classrooms but also to foster environments that are deeply engaging and conducive to higher levels of student engagement and motivation. By carefully aligning AI capabilities with pedagogical goals, we can create a dynamic educational landscape that is responsive to the needs of all learners and poised for the future.

Let's start by examining the principles of AI, which are foundational to understanding its ethical and effective use. Establishing these principles is crucial, as they guide how AI technologies are integrated and utilized, ensuring they serve educational purposes responsibly and beneficially.

AI Principles

When it comes to blending AI into our classrooms, I believe there are a few key principles that we educators should keep in mind. Based on the ideas from international guidelines from Australia, UNESCO, Singapore, the European Commission, and the U.S. Department of Defense, as well as my own research into the fast-changing world of AI technology, I've distilled AI guidelines and crafted a set of five key AI principles that I believe are essential for the educational sector as illustrated in figure 5.1

Figure 5.1:

5 AI Principles

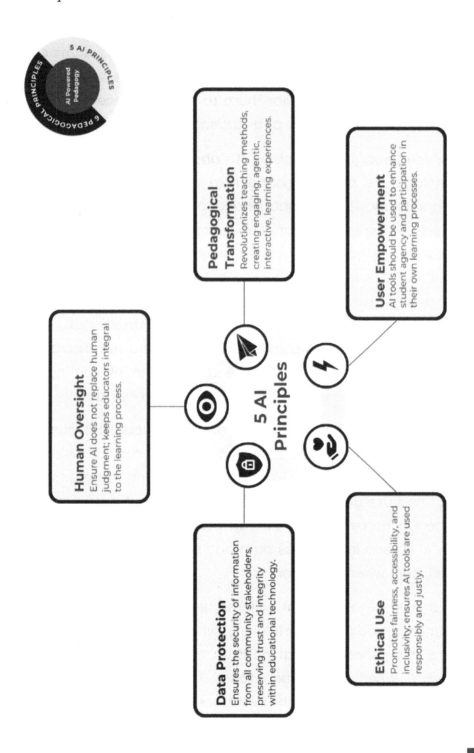

I believe these aren't just guidelines; they're essential foundations for creating a learning environment that's not only enhanced by technology but also deeply rooted in human values. By pulling together the best practices and insights from different systems from around the world, I've aimed to create a holistic and adaptable approach that ensures AI is used safely, ethically, and effectively in schools. This process allowed me to harness global insights and tailor them to meet the specific needs and challenges of today's educators and students.

Let me talk you through this decision. It's about more than just keeping up with technology. It's about steering it in a direction that upholds our principles and supports our educational goals. For instance, by insisting on *human oversight*, we ensure that AI doesn't replace the invaluable human touch in education but works alongside it, enhancing the educational process without overriding it. The key here is to maintain your human judgment; always use your professional judgment when interpreting AI-generated recommendations and making instructional decisions. Remember that AI should complement, not replace, human interaction and instruction. Always retain the ultimate authority in evaluating student learning and making decisions about their educational journey.

Data protection is another major area of focus because it builds trust—everyone involved in education, from students to faculty, needs to feel confident that their personal information is safe and handled with care. Only collect and use the minimum amount of student data necessary for the AI tool to function effectively. Be transparent with students and parents about how AI is used in the classroom and what data is collected. Obtain informed consent when necessary.

Educators should be aware that children under 13 are entitled to specific data protection measures, particularly when using AI tools. To ensure compliance, it is advisable that children are not required to input any personal data when using such tools. The General Data Protection Regulation (GDPR) emphasizes the need for clear and plain language when communicating with children to ensure their understanding of how their data will be used. Additionally, the UK's Data Protection Act 2018 sets the age limit for children's consent to data processing in the context of online services at 13 years.

Therefore, educators should take steps to ensure that AI tools used by children under 13 do not collect their personal data, and if data input is necessary, parental consent should be obtained.

> **Practical Tip: Enhance Privacy in AI Learning for Young Students**
>
> *For children under 13, set up interactive learning stations using devices logged into school accounts. This centralizes AI tool access on shared classroom devices, ensuring student privacy and complying with age restrictions, without requiring personal information. This method not only boosts digital learning security but also creates a safe, engaging environment that aligns with data protection standards.*

Understanding Data Collection Practices

One of the primary ethical concerns regarding AI in education is the collection and use of student data. AI tools often require access to various data points, such as student performance, and even personal information, to function effectively. While this data can be invaluable for learning experiences, it also raises concerns about student privacy and data security.

The first step toward responsible data stewardship is understanding what data AI tools collect and how this data is used. Educators should carefully review the privacy policies and terms of service of any AI tool before implementation.

Key questions to consider include are included in figure 5.2

Figure 5.2:

Data Collection

DATA COLLECTION

1 **WHAT TYPES OF STUDENT DATA ARE COLLECTED?**
This includes academic performance, demographic information, and other relevant data.

2 **HOW IS THE DATA USED?**
Determine if the data is solely for learning or also used for research, marketing, or other purposes.

3 **WHO HAS ACCESS TO THE DATA?**
Identify if the data is shared with third-party companies or organizations.

4 **HOW IS THE DATA SECURED?**
Understand the methods used to protect the data from unauthorized access.

5 **WHAT MEASURES ARE IN PLACE TO PROTECT DATA FROM BREACHES?**
Explore the specific security protocols and safeguards implemented.

Compliance with Data Privacy Regulations

Educators must ensure that their use of AI tools complies with relevant data privacy regulations, such as the Family Educational Rights and Privacy Act (FERPA) in the United States and the General Data Protection Regulation (GDPR) in Europe. These regulations provide guidelines for the collection, use, and disclosure of student data. Familiarizing yourself with these regulations and ensuring your chosen AI tools adhere to them is essential.

Data Security Measures

Protecting student data from unauthorized access and breaches is paramount. Figure 5.3 outlines some of key data security measures to consider.

Figure 5.3:

Data Security Measures

Implement strong password policies and multi-factor authentication for accessing student data, ensuring robust security measures are in place. Ensure that student data is encrypted both in transit and at rest to protect it from unauthorized access. Keep AI tools and operating systems up-to-date with the latest security patches by conducting regular software updates. Practice data minimization by collecting only the minimum amount of student data necessary for the AI tool to function effectively. Store student data on secure servers and limit access to authorized personnel only, maintaining the confidentiality and integrity of the information.

The next AI principle, *ethical use*, ensures that the AI tools we use are fair and don't perpetuate biases or stereotypes, which helps us maintain a fair and just learning environment. This principle is also about teaching students about responsible and ethical AI use and academic integrity and honesty. A more in-depth discussion on developing ethical learners can be found in chapter eight.

Empowering users is a foundational AI principle that emphasizes enhancing student agency and participation in their own learning processes. AI should be leveraged to boost students' creativity and give them greater ownership over their educational journey. AI can provide a more interactive learning environment and help students develop a deeper understanding and mastery of the subjects they are studying. By empowering students with AI, we can create a more dynamic and student-centered educational experience.

Finally we have *transforming pedagogy*—a principle all about using AI to change the way we teach, making learning more engaging and agentic for every student. This principle encourages technology adoption at the upper two levels of the SAMR model—Modification and Redefinition—proposed by Dr. Ruben Puentedura (2010) as seen here in figure 5.4. These levels are considered transformative, as they enable educators to not just enhance their teaching methods with technology but to fundamentally alter how learning occurs. In the Modification stage, technology allows for significant task redesign, enhancing how students engage with material.

The Redefinition stage leverages technology to create new tasks that were previously inconceivable. Under this principle, educators can utilize AI tools to innovate and push boundaries in curriculum design and delivery, thereby fostering a learning environment that is not only more interactive and engaging but also tailored to meet the diverse needs and potentials of all students. This approach aligns seamlessly with the transformative goals of the SAMR model, promoting a deeper, more impactful integration of technology in education.

Figure 5.3 illustrates the SAMR while figure 5.4 provides AI examples for each SAMR level.

Figure 5.4:

SAMR Technology Integration Model

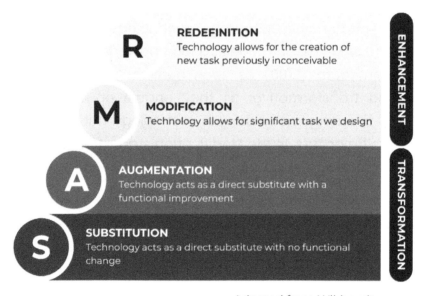

The SAMR Model
Dr. Ruben Puentedura

R REDEFINITION
Technology allows for the creation of new task previously inconceivable

M MODIFICATION
Technology allows for significant task we design

A AUGMENTATION
Technology acts as a direct substitute with a functional improvement

S SUBSTITUTION
Technology acts as a direct substitute with no functional change

ENHANCEMENT

TRANSFORMATION

Adapted from Wikiversity

Figure 5.5:

AI Examples for Each SAMR level

Enhancement	Substitution	Technology acts as a direct substitute with no functional change	Using AI tools to generate long boring lectures and worksheets.
	Augmentation	Technology acts as a direct substitute with a functional improvement	AI tools can support grammar and spelling in writing tasks. Voice to text tools can transcribe information more efficiently
	Modification	Technology allows for significant task we design	Data Analysis Projects: Students can use AI tools to analyze large datasets in subjects like social science, biology, or economics. For instance, AI can help students identify patterns and correlations in climate change data, enabling them to propose evidence-based solutions. Enhanced Reading Assistance: AI can support students who struggle with reading by providing real-time assistance. This could include reading aloud text, explaining difficult words or phrases, and highlighting key information in texts, thus making reading more accessible and engaging. Multimedia Content Analysis: AI tools can aid students in analyzing multimedia content, such as videos, podcasts, and images. For instance, AI can automatically transcribe video lectures, highlight important points, and analyze sentiment in documentaries or debates, enriching the learning experience and accessibility.
Transformation	Redefinition	Technology allows for the creation of new task previously inconceivable	AI as a Creative Partner in Art and Music: In art and music education, AI can act as a creative partner by suggesting modifications to designs or compositions, or by generating ideas for creative exploration. For example, AI could suggest alterations to a student's musical composition based on the style they are studying, or it could generate starter sketches that students can then expand into detailed artworks. AI in Debate and Argumentation Training: AI can be programmed to debate with students on a variety of topics, using vast databases to argue from different perspectives. This would not only enhance critical thinking skills but also prepare students for public speaking and logical reasoning in a novel, interactive format. AI-driven Role Plays and Simulations: In subjects like history or political science, AI can simulate historical figures or governmental bodies, allowing students to role-play scenarios such as international negotiations or historical events. This redefines learning by creating immersive, interactive experiences that were previously not possible.

Pedagogical Principles

In developing a pedagogical framework for this book, I've drawn inspiration from several educational principles that align closely with those adopted by prestigious programs such as the International Baccalaureate (IB), known for its holistic educational approach. The principles I focus on include the following:

Teaching is concept based, inquiry based, inclusive and equitable, collaborative, learner centered, and learner driven, and learning is evidenced as seen in figure 5.6. Each of these has been selected for their ability to create an engaging and effective learning environment.

Concept-based learning is central to encouraging students to think critically and understand complex concepts deeply, enabling learners to apply and transfer their understanding to new, varied contexts, preparing them for real-world challenges and unfamiliar situations.

"Concept-based curriculum and instruction is a three-dimensional design model that frames factual content and skills with disciplinary concepts, generalizations, and principles" (Erickson, 2007).

Concept-based curriculum and instruction stands in contrast to the traditional two-dimensional topic-based curriculum, which primarily focuses on factual content and skills but often only implicitly addresses the development of conceptual understanding and the transfer of knowledge, rather than doing so intentionally.

Inquiry-based learning invites students to pose questions and explore the different pathways, fostering a sense of exploration and discovery. Kath Murdoch (2014), the leading global expert on inquiry-based learning, outlines 13 core principles of the inquiry teacher's practice: ownership, interest, reflection, purpose, prior learning, transfer, collaboration, resilience, time, feedback, environment, openness, and, most importantly, joy.

The principle of *inclusivity and equity* ensures that education is accessible to all students, reflecting a commitment to honoring the strengths and talents of each and every student (e.g., neurodiverse learners) within the learning environment.

Collaborative learning complements this by promoting teamwork, where students learn from and with each other, enhancing their interpersonal skills and their ability to work within diverse groups.

Adopting a *learner-centered* and *learner-driven* approach means that teaching strategies are tailored to meet the student's passions and interests, placing them at the very core of the learning cycle. This principle also encompasses the idea of *constructivism*, where learners build their own understanding and knowledge of the world by experiencing things and reflecting on those experiences.

Finally, the practice of teachers *collecting evidence of learning* is crucial for continually assessing student progress. This not only helps in providing targeted feedback but also in refining teaching methods to better suit the evolving needs of students.

These pedagogical principles are not just theoretical ideals; they are practical tools that have been shown to foster an enriching and dynamic educational environment. By integrating these into our educational approach, we aim to equip students with the skills necessary to navigate and succeed in an increasingly complex world.

Figure 5.6:
6 Pedagogical Principles

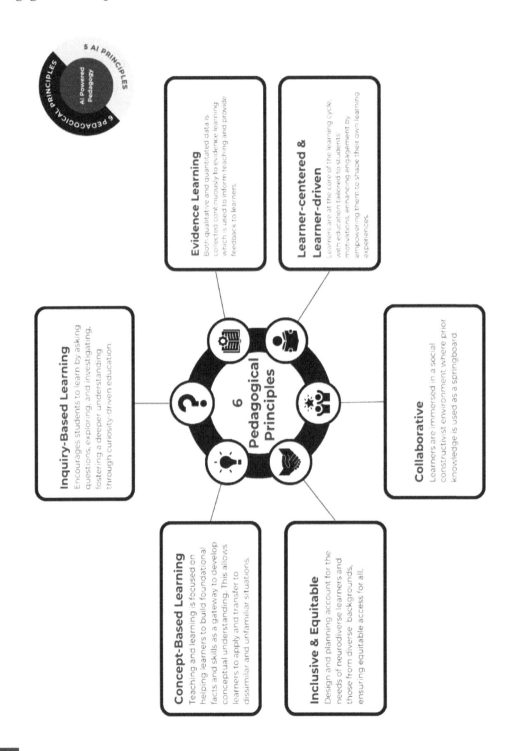

Figure 5.7:

AI-Powered Pedagogy

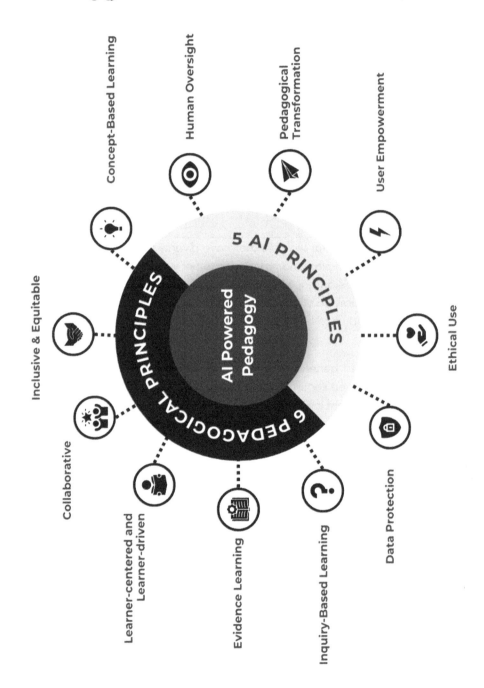

Examples from the Classroom

Here are examples of how different educators have integrated AI with the pedagogical principles.

Case Study 1: AI use in Grade 2 – Inquiry into Sustainability and Preservation of Resources

Pedagogical principle:

- Inclusive & equitable
- Evidenced learning

I used AI to generate scaffolds for learners that have diverse language needs. Using AI is a game changer. During the co-planning process, together with the EAL specialist teacher, we focused on sentence frames and opinion writing. Then, we generated more simplified and complex versions of the same scaffold, making planning for differentiated instruction much more efficient. This allowed us to have a stack of options available to meet students where they were at.

Using AI has allowed us to generate tailored language scaffolds for all students in the classroom, which has boosted English language learners' confidence as a result. "Oh, other students get help too? I thought it was only me, because my English is not good."

Juan Carlos Cairós

Amazing PYP inquiry teacher

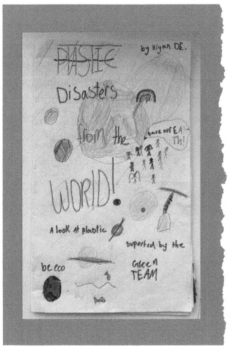

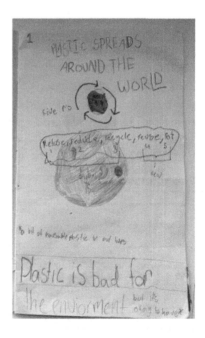

Another example of AI use

Case Study 2: AI Use in the IB MYP Personal Project

Pedagogical principles:

- Concept-based learning
- Inquiry-based learning
- Inclusive and equitable
- Learner centered and learner driven

My MYP personal project was a response to a need that I identified in Cambodia, where I live. I developed a website with training on allergies such as gluten, lactose, and milk products. The courses are aimed at people who work at restaurants and can potentially enable cross-contamination. As a celiac, I had prior knowledge about gluten, but I needed to do a lot more research about lactose and milk products. I used generative AI to do research and come up with a proposed website structure, which I adjusted to my needs. Then I compared the information obtained and chose what I was most interested in and thought would meet my customers' needs. I find AI useful as a way to gain inertia and materialize ideas that I have, and then mold and develop them in the way I consider appropriate. Improving my prompt generation skills has been instrumental in making the best out of this technology.

Here is my website (below).

Pablo Cairós, grade 10 student

Specialized Courses on Food Allergies

These specialized courses are designed to educate waiters and chefs about food allergies, with a focus on gluten allergies and special diets. The courses provide in-depth knowledge and practical strategies for serving customers with specific dietary requirements.

Importance of Educating Waiters and Chefs

Case Study 3: Grade 5 IB PYP Exhibition

 Pedagogical principles:

- Concept-based learning
- Inquiry-based learning
- Inclusive and equitable
- Learner centered and learner driven

This was the first year we had AI tools to help us in the PYP Exhibition, and it was revolutionary. As a class, we spent time exploring some AI tools, recognizing their usefulness, and finding some limitations; after that, students were able to confidently use AI in their learning journey. Tools such as summarizing a video/article and text rewriter allowed every student access to higher-level articles or videos with great detail about their topic. Students could then differentiate the information to a level that they could engage with. It allows information to be tailored to the specific needs of the students. Normally, as a teacher, that takes me hours after school to organize, but with AI tools it can happen in real time, in class, catering to the specific questions or needs of a student. It equips students to drive their learning in ways that were not possible before. Like I said, revolutionary.

Here are four grade 5 students' quotes around the process:

- "It was super helpful for sorting ideas and resources."
- "I got AI to prepare questions for me to answer so when I had a live audience for the presentation, I was ready."
- "AI was really useful and helped me expand my thinking around gaming addiction."
- "AI helped me find many sources and ways to explore my thinking around aggression in football that I haven't had before."

Michael Parkin

PYP Educator

Figure 5.8:

Pedagogical Mistakes with AI Use

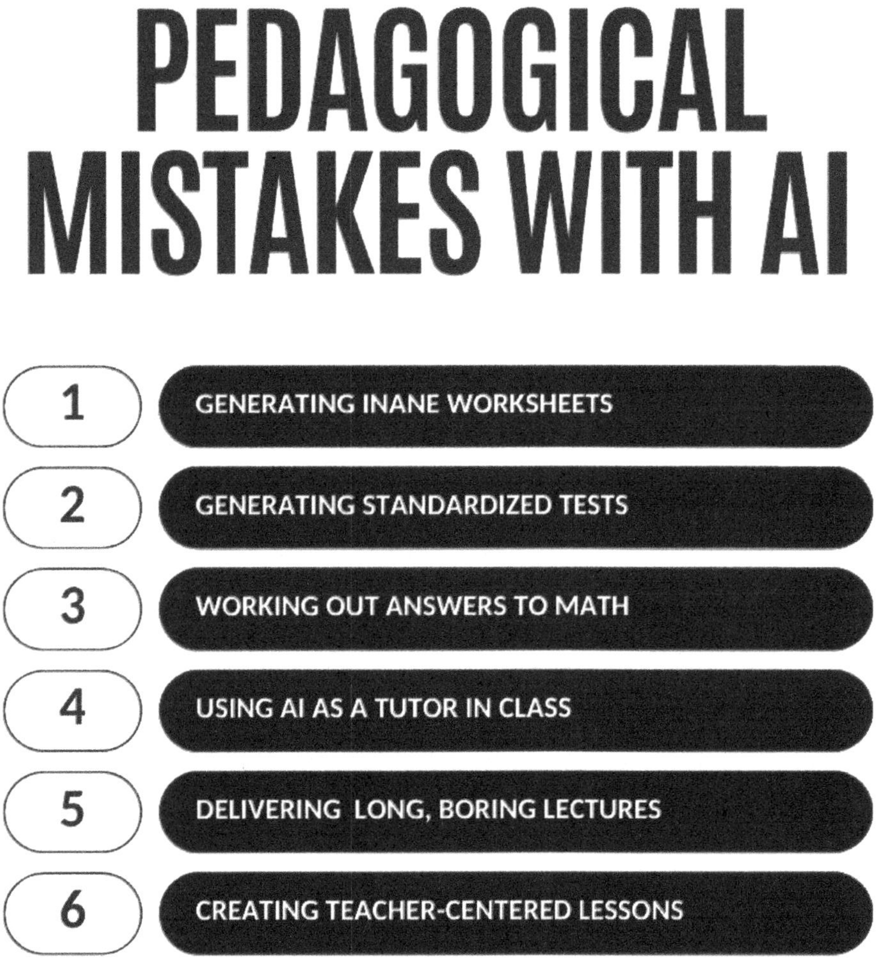

PEDAGOGICAL MISTAKES WITH AI

1	GENERATING INANE WORKSHEETS
2	GENERATING STANDARDIZED TESTS
3	WORKING OUT ANSWERS TO MATH
4	USING AI AS A TUTOR IN CLASS
5	DELIVERING LONG, BORING LECTURES
6	CREATING TEACHER-CENTERED LESSONS

Figure 5.8 highlights some common pedagogical pitfalls educators may encounter when integrating AI into their teaching practices. We must be mindful of avoiding approaches that reduce AI to a mere automation tool for generating inane worksheets, standardized tests with shallow multiple-choice questions, or rote memorization. Such practices not only fail to leverage the transformative potential of AI but also risk perpetuating outdated, passive learning models that stifle creativity and critical thinking.

Additionally, placing undue emphasis on the value of AI as an in-class tutor can detract from the benefits of social constructivism, where collaborative learning and interaction drive student conceptual understanding and engagement. Relying on AI to help deliver long, monotonous lectures or create teacher-centered lessons rather than focusing on student-driven and student-centered approaches can undermine the potential of AI to enhance meaningful and interactive learning experiences.

Chapter Summary

This chapter explored the integration of AI into education to encourage a move from traditional teacher-centric methods to student-centered, inquiry-based approaches. The chapter introduces a set of fundamental AI principles—*human oversight*, *data protection*, *ethical use*, *user empowerment*, and *pedagogical transformation*. These principles are drawn from international guidelines and tailored to ensure that AI is used safely, ethically, and effectively in educational settings. These principles ensure AI's safe, ethical, and effective use in classrooms, emphasizing that AI should augment rather than replace human teaching elements and maintaining educators' central role in the learning process.

The chapter also discussed how these AI principles should be harmonized with established pedagogical principles where learning is concept based, inquiry based, inclusive and equitable, collaborative, and evidenced. These pedagogical principles foster an environment where students are encouraged to explore, question, and collaborate, thereby deepening their understanding and engagement.

Practical examples of AI integration in education are provided, including its application in various grade levels and subjects, demonstrating how AI can support and enhance pedagogical principles in real-world settings.

Discussion Questions

1. Data Protection Concerns: Considering the emphasis on data protection, discuss how educators can balance the need for utilizing AI tools with the imperative to protect student data. What are the best practices for ensuring data privacy while fostering a learning environment enriched by AI?

2. Pedagogical Transformation Principle: Reflect on the pedagogical transformation principle, which aims to fundamentally change teaching methods. Can you provide examples from your own experience where AI has successfully transformed pedagogical practices? If not, what barriers have prevented this transformation?

3. Harmonizing AI and Pedagogical Principles: Discuss how the harmonization of AI principles with pedagogical principles can enhance the design of learning experiences and units of inquiry. What are some practical strategies educators can use to ensure that AI tools are not just supplementary but integral to achieving pedagogical goals?

Artefact Opportunity

Integrate AI with Pedagogy:

Identify a professional development area that you would like to explore. Ensure you focus on how AI tools can be integrated into your teaching practices while aligning with one of the pedagogical principles discussed in the chapter (e.g., inquiry-based learning). Develop an action plan for your professional development needs.

CHAPTER 6
CRAFTING EFFECTIVE PROMPTS

In the realm of AI, the quality of your questions
shapes the depth of your discoveries.
—GPT-4o, 2024

How Can Educators Move Beyond Static Prompt Libraries and Embrace the Art of Crafting and Iteratively Refining Prompts to Achieve More Meaningful and Conversational Interactions with AI Tools?

By now, many of us have realized that the ongoing conversation with any AI tool is necessary to refine and sift through the outputs to extract the little nuggets of gold. There is no such thing as the perfect AI prompt that gives the perfect output.

AI PROMPTS

1. **YOU DON'T NEED A PROMPT LIBRARY**

2. **CONDUCT AN ONGOING CONVERSATION**

3. **USE THE I.D.E.A.S. FRAMEWORK**

Therefore, when crafting prompts, it's essential to view the process as an ongoing, dynamic conversation rather than a static collection of entries in a prompt library. Each conversation should be seen as a starting point for dialogue, exploration, and discovery, evolving based on the output of the AI tool. Relying heavily on a pre-set prompt library is cumbersome and time-consuming. While some templates may

Image generated by DALL·E 3, 2024

provide a helpful starting point, where does it end? Additionally, managing an overly large prompt library is not very practical. It forces educators to waste valuable time digging through countless options.

Large language models (LLMs) inherently fall under the broad category of natural language processing (NLP), which means they are designed to understand and generate natural, conversational language. Therefore, instead of relying on a rigid, predefined set of prompts, it's more effective to engage with these models using fluid and natural language to tap into their full potential.

By thinking about interactions with AI tools as an ongoing conversation, we can generate the most effective and relevant outputs. This approach allows for continuous adaptation and refinement, ensuring that the dialogue remains productive and aligned with the desired outcome.

In one of my blog posts, titled "Is Prompt Engineering Really Prompt 'Engineering?'", I delved into the nuanced world of AI interaction, exploring the misnomer "prompt engineering." Unlike traditional engineering, which relies heavily on fixed scientific and mathematical principles, prompt development in the context of AI is not really engineering per se. I argue that it is less about rigid sciences and more akin to having an ongoing conversation with a thought partner.

In my blog, I describe developing prompts as an iterative process where each adjustment to the prompt isn't just random but is a refined, thoughtful tweak toward achieving clearer and more effective communication with AI. This iterative development, inspired by the design thinking process, highlights the ongoing conversation between the user and the AI, aiming to enhance the coherence and effectiveness of the AI's responses.

Despite experimenting with numerous existing frameworks and various tools designed for developing prompts, I have found that none have stuck with me for one reason or another. During one of our regular hikes, my dear friend Haihao introduced me to a blog post by Lance Cummings that explained the application of the rhetorical triangle in enhancing prompt construction. Inspired by this, I've integrated these concepts and explored the five canons of rhetoric, endeavoring to devise a more intuitive and impactful approach to prompt development that reflects the iterative and refinement process when communicating with any AI.

The <u>five canons or tenets of rhetoric,</u> as articulated by the Roman orator Cicero, are *Inventio* (Invention), *Dispositio* (Arrangement), *Elocutio* (Style), *Memoria* (Memory), and *Pronuntiatio* and *Actio* (Presentation and Delivery). Originally these tenets were created to develop public speaking and reflect the iterative nature of writing that incorporates the stages of drafting, writing, and rewriting as a cyclical process.

From Wikipedia (2023):

Rhetorical education focused on five <u>canons</u>. The Five Canons of Rhetoric serve as a guide to creating persuasive messages and arguments:

- **Inventio** (Invention): the process that leads to the development and refinement of an argument.
- **Dispositio** (Disposition or Arrangement): used to determine how an argument should be organized for greatest effect, usually beginning with the <u>exordium</u>.
- **Elocutio** (Style): determining how to present the arguments.
- **Memoria** (Memory): the process of learning and memorizing the speech and persuasive messages.
- **Pronuntiatio** (Presentation) and <u>Actio</u> (Delivery): the gestures, pronunciation, tone, and pace used when presenting the persuasive arguments—the <u>Grand Style</u>.

Based on these *ideas* (literally), I have created an acronym that may help with AI prompt development that operates in two stages to reflect the iterative refinement nature of crafting prompts. The I.D.E.A.S. framework stands for Inquire, Design, Engage, Adapt, and Synthesize and is used to guide the process of prompting.

The initial steps of input involve inquiring, designing, and engaging. Once a response is received, the next phase is to adapt and synthesize the output.

I.D.E.A.S. emphasizes a structured yet flexible approach to crafting prompts that are not only functional but also intuitive and impactful. Figure 6.1 summarizes the key points about I.D.E.A.S.

Figure 6.1:

I.D.E.A.S. for AI Prompt Development

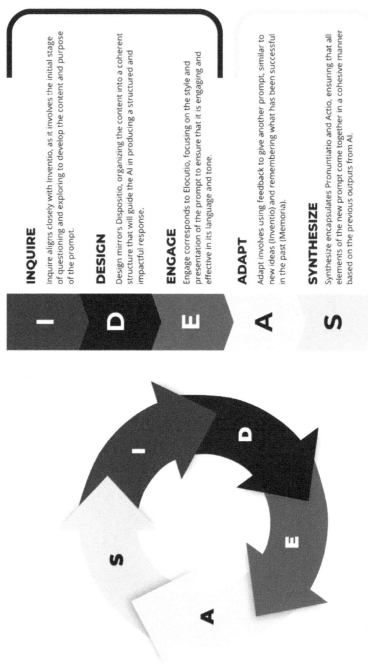

I.D.E.A.S. for AI Prompt Development

ADAPTED FROM THE 5 CANONS OF RHETORIC

INQUIRE

Inquire aligns closely with Inventio, as it involves the initial stage of questioning and exploring to develop the content and purpose of the prompt.

DESIGN

Design mirrors Dispositio, organizing the content into a coherent structure that will guide the AI in producing a structured and impactful response.

ENGAGE

Engage corresponds to Elocutio, focusing on the style and presentation of the prompt to ensure that it is engaging and effective in its language and tone.

ADAPT

Adapt involves using feedback to give another prompt, similar to new ideas (Inventio) and remembering what has been successful in the past (Memoria).

SYNTHESIZE

Synthesize encapsulates Pronuntiatio and Actio, ensuring that all elements of the new prompt come together in a cohesive manner based on the previous outputs from AI.

www.jenniferchangwathall.com

JCW

IDEAS emphasizes starting with a deep inquiry into the needs and context, designing a coherent prompt, engaging actively with the AI, adapting based on feedback, and specifying necessary adjustments for continual improvement.

Through this framework, I advocate for a more dynamic, responsive approach to communicating with AI—one that moves beyond a mere library of static prompts to a more vibrant, interactive crafting process that evolves with each user interaction. This approach ensures that AI's generative responses are contextually appropriate, providing meaningful and impactful educational experiences.

Figure 6.2 provides some questions we may ask as we are going through the IDEAS framework:

Figure 6.2:

Questions for the I.D.E.A.S. Framework

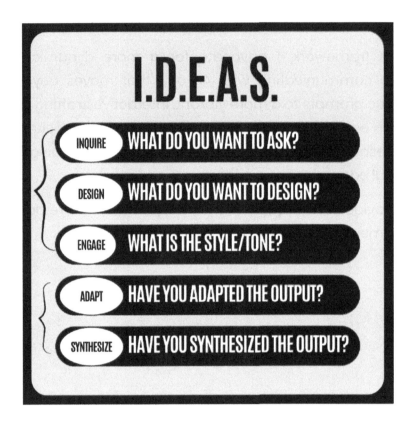

Practical Tip: Think of AI Tools as Experienced and Wise Teachers

Treat AI tools as wise, experienced teachers that have a vast reservoir of knowledge and insights to share.

Just as you would ask a seasoned educator for their perspective on a challenging topic, approach AI with thoughtful questions that invite exploration and discussion. This shifts the mindset of the interaction from simply retrieving information to engaging in a meaningful dialogue that can lead to better suggestions and ideas.

By treating AI as a collaborative partner in the educational process, you can harness its full potential to enhance your teaching strategies, inspire creativity, and foster a richer learning environment for your students.

Here Are Some Examples of How We Can Use the I.D.E.A.S. Framework:

1. Developing a Math Unit of Inquiry for Grade 6

Inquire: Design: Engage:

@GPT-4
Inquire
Can you come up with a 6th-grade project-based learning unit on fractions focusing on equivalent fractions, addition, and comparison and probability?
Design
Outline the unit and include interactive inductive, inquiry-based lessons with an engaging intro to fractions, a hands-on activity for exploring equivalency, and a practical application for adding and comparing fractions. Include metacognition prompts and main active learning experiences. Can you include guiding questions and give me four weeks' worth of inductive learning experiences and also include a culminating authentic performance task with a rubric in the table?
Engage
In this unit design, the fractions need to be relatable and exciting for 11-year-olds, cultivating curiosity and interaction in the classroom.

From GPT-4-128k on Poe:
https://poe.com/s/OYWn52VQGIJpEJ2sHvRM

Four-Week Project-Based Learning Unit on Fractions for 6th Grade

Unit Overview:

This unit focuses on helping 6th-grade students understand and apply key concepts regarding fractions, such as equivalent fractions, fraction addition, comparison, and an introduction to probability using fractions. The unit is designed to be engaging, hands-on, and relevant, using inquiry-based methods to foster curiosity and active learning.

Week 1: Introduction to Fractions and Exploring Equivalence

Goal: Students will understand what fractions represent and begin exploring equivalent fractions.

-Day 1: Engaging Introduction

- Activity: "Fraction of Your World." Students take photos or bring in items that show fractions in real life (e.g., a half-eaten apple, a quarter of a pizza).
- Discussion: "What are fractions? Why do we use them?"

-Days 2–4: Exploring Equivalence

- Activity: "Fraction Art." Students use colored paper to create visual representations of equivalent fractions.
- Metacognition Prompt: "How did creating visual representations help you understand equivalent fractions?"
- Guiding Questions: "How can two different-looking pieces represent the same fraction?"

-Day 5: Reflection and Sharing

- Activity: Students present their fraction art and explain why the fractions are equivalent.
- Guiding Question: "What strategies helped you identify equivalent fractions?"

Week 2: Addition of Fractions

Goal: Students will learn to add fractions with like and unlike denominators.

- -Days 1–2: Introduction to Adding Fractions
- Activity: "Fraction Bakery." Using real recipes, students adjust quantities by adding fractions together.
- Hands-On: Simulation of recipe adjustment in class.
- Guiding Question: "What do we need to remember when adding fractions with unlike denominators?"

-Days 3-4: Application through Simulation

- Activity: "Picnic Prep." Plan a picnic where students must calculate the food needed using fraction addition.
- Metacognition Prompt: "How did adjusting the quantities help you understand fraction addition?"
- Guiding Question: "How does fraction addition help in real-life situations like cooking?"

-Day 5: Group Discussions and Reflection

- Activity: Students discuss the challenges and strategies used in the picnic prep simulation.
- Guiding Question: "Share a tip or strategy that helped you with the addition of fractions."

Week 3: Comparing and Ordering Fractions

Goal: Students will compare and order fractions through practical applications.

-Days 1-2: Fraction Comparison Activities

- Activity: "Fraction Race." Using number lines on the floor, students place themselves according to fraction cards they receive.

- Interactive: Fraction card games to deepen understanding of ordering.
- Guiding Questions: "Which strategies can we use to decide which fraction is larger?"

-Days 3–4: Real-Life Application

- Activity: "Classroom Supplies Sort-Out." Dividing classroom supplies using fractions.
- Metacognition Prompt: "What challenges did you face while dividing the supplies, and how did you overcome them?"
- Guiding Question: "How can comparing fractions be useful when dividing items or resources?"

-Day 5: Culminating Discussion

- Activity: Reflective discussion on the importance of accurate fraction comparison.
- Guiding Question: "What real-life situations might require you to compare fractions?"

Week 4: Introduction to Probability with Fractions

Goal: Apply understanding of fractions to basic probability concepts.

-Days 1–2: Basic Probability Concepts

- Activity: "Fractional Probability." Simple experiments (e.g., rolling dice, drawing cards) to calculate probability.
- Guiding Question: "How can we express probability as a fraction?"

-Days 3–4: Conducting a Survey

- Activity: Students design and conduct a survey, analyzing results using fractions.
- Metacognition Prompt: "What did the survey results teach you about probability and fractions?"
- Guiding Question: "How can understanding fractions improve our interpretation of data?"

-Day 5: Culminating Project and Presentation

- Activity: Groups present their survey findings and explain the probability concepts learned.
- Guiding Question: "How did fractions enhance our understanding of probability?"

Culminating Performance Task:

Task: Students will plan and execute a small event (like a school fair booth) where they must use their knowledge of fractions to divide resources, budget expenses, and analyze the success probability of games or activities.

Performance Task Rubric:

Criteria	Excellent (4)	Good (3)	Satisfactory (2)	Needs Improvement (1)

| Understanding Fractions | Demonstrates a clear understanding of fractions in planning and execution. | Shows basic understanding but makes minor errors in calculations. | Struggles to apply fractions correctly; frequent errors. | Lacks understanding of how to use fractions in practical scenarios. |

| Application of Addition & Comparison | Accurately adds and compares fractions in all planning aspects. | Generally accurate but with occasional miscalculations. | Frequent inaccuracies in addition or comparison of fractions. | Fails to add or compare fractions accurately, affecting planning. |

| Use of Probability | Uses probability effectively to predict outcomes and make decisions. | Uses basic probability concepts correctly most of the time. | Limited use of probability, with some misunderstanding. | Does not incorporate probability or misuses it entirely. |

| Presentation and Explanation | Presents findings clearly, explaining the use of fractions and probability with confidence. | Presentation is coherent, with minor lapses in clarity or detail. | Presentation lacks clarity or detail in explaining fractions and probability. | Unable to clearly explain how fractions and probability were used. |

Reflection and Metacognition:

Throughout the unit, students will be encouraged to think about their learning process and the practical applications of fractions. Each week, they should reflect on:

- What concepts were easy or difficult to understand and why.
- How the hands-on activities helped clarify or confuse their understanding.
- How they can apply the week's learning in real-world scenarios.

This approach not only reinforces the mathematical concepts but also enhances students' ability to self-assess and direct their own learning processes.

After the Inquire, Design, and Engage (IDE) stages, we read the AI generated output. Then we use the next stages: Adapt and Synthesize to continue the conversation with the AI tool. You can see here that the formatting of the rubric makes the output difficult to follow, so my next prompt was as follows:

@GPT-4 Can you put the rubric in a table?

Retrieved from GPT-4 https://poe.com/s/9iaocJpjVOFsISuyLFKo, 2024

Criteria	Excellent (4)	Good (3)	Satisfactory (2)	Needs Improvement (1)
Understanding Fractions	Demonstrates a clear understanding of fractions in planning and execution.	Shows basic understanding but makes minor errors in calculations.	Struggles to apply fractions correctly; frequent errors.	Lacks understanding of how to use fractions in practical scenarios.
Application of Addition & Comparison	Accurately adds and compares fractions in all planning aspects.	Generally accurate but with occasional miscalculations.	Frequent inaccuracies in addition or comparison of fractions.	Fails to add or compare fractions accurately, affecting planning.
Use of Probability	Uses probability effectively to predict outcomes and make decisions.	Uses basic probability concepts correctly most of the time.	Limited use of probability, with some misunderstanding.	Does not incorporate probability or misuses it entirely.
Presentation and Explanation	Presents findings clearly, explaining the use of fractions and probability with confidence.	Presentation is coherent, with minor lapses in clarity or detail.	Presentation lacks clarity or detail in explaining fractions and probability.	Unable to clearly explain how fractions and probability were used.

2. Developing a Unit of Inquiry on Living Things for Grade 2

> **@GPT-4o**
> **Inquire**
> Can you come up with a 2nd-grade project-based learning unit on living things including plants and animals.
> **Design**
> Outline the unit and include interactive inductive, inquiry-based lessons with an engaging intro to living things and a hands-on activity for exploring. Include metacognition prompts and main active learning experiences. Can you include guiding questions and give me four weeks' worth of inductive learning experiences and also include a culminating authentic performance task with a rubric in a table?
> **Engage**
> In this unit design, livings things need to be relatable and exciting for second graders, cultivating curiosity and interaction in the classroom.

Retrieved from GPT-4o https://poe.com/s/nVLKZJ3usEy7cw3I5JA4, *2024*

2nd Grade Project-Based Learning Unit: Living Things (Plants and Animals)

Unit Overview

This four-week unit will delve into the fascinating world of plants and animals. Through interactive, inquiry-based lessons and hands-on activities, students will gain a deep understanding of living things. The unit will include metacognitive prompts and active learning experiences to cultivate students' curiosity and interaction. The unit will culminate in an authentic performance task where students will showcase their learning.

Week 1: Introduction to Living Things

Objective: Students will understand the basic characteristics of living things and differentiate between living and non-living things.

Day 1: Engaging Introduction

- Activity: Watch an engaging video about living things (e.g., animals, plants).
- Discussion: What makes something alive? How can we tell the difference between living and non-living things?

Day 2: Characteristics of Living Things

- Interactive Lesson: Create a chart listing characteristics of living things (growth, reproduction, response to environment, etc.).
- Hands-On Activity: Students bring in objects from home (or choose from the classroom) and classify them as living or non-living.

Day 3: Inquiry-Based Exploration

- Guiding Questions:
- How do living things grow?
- What do living things need to survive?
- Activity: Plant seeds in small pots and predict what will happen.

Day 4: Metacognition Prompt

- Prompt: "Think about the objects you classified. Why did you decide they were living or non-living? Write down your thoughts."

Day 5: Active Learning Experience

- Activity: Nature walk to observe living and non-living things in the schoolyard.
- Discussion: Share observations and discuss the characteristics of the living things they saw.

Week 2: Plants

Objective: Students will learn about the basic parts of plants and their functions and understand the life cycle of a plant.

Day 1: Engaging Introduction

- Activity: Read a storybook about plants and their parts.
- Discussion: What are the parts of a plant? What do they do?

Day 2: Inquiry-Based Exploration

- Guiding Questions:
- How do plants grow?
- What do plants need to survive?
- Activity: Observe the seeds planted in week 1 and document changes.

Day 3: Interactive Lesson

- Activity: Create a diagram of a plant and label the parts (root, stem, leaf, flower).
- Hands-On Activity: Dissect a flower and identify its parts.

Day 4: Metacognition Prompt

- Prompt: "Think about the plants you see every day. How do they grow and change? Write down your observations."

Day 5: Active Learning Experience

- Activity: Plant an outdoor garden (if possible) or start a classroom windowsill garden.
- Discussion: Predict what will happen to the plants over the next few weeks.

Week 3: Animals

Objective: Students will learn about different types of animals, their habitats, and their basic needs.

Day 1: Engaging Introduction

- Activity: Watch a documentary clip about different animals and their habitats.
- Discussion: What animals do you know? Where do they live?

Day 2: Inquiry-Based Exploration

- Guiding Questions:
- How do animals find food?
- What do animals need to survive?
- Activity: Create a habitat diorama for a classroom pet or a favorite animal.

Day 3: Interactive Lesson

- Activity: Classify animals into groups (mammals, birds, reptiles, etc.) using pictures and models.
- Hands-On Activity: Compare and contrast different animal groups using a Venn diagram.

Day 4: Metacognition Prompt

- Prompt: "Think about an animal you learned about this week. What makes it special? How is it different from other animals?"

Day 5: Active Learning Experience

- Activity: Animal role-play. Students choose an animal and act out how it moves, eats, and lives.
- Discussion: Reflect on the different ways animals live and survive.

Week 4: Integration and Synthesis

Objective: Students will integrate their knowledge of plants and animals to understand ecosystems and the interdependence of living things.

Day 1: Engaging Introduction

-   Activity: Watch a video on ecosystems and food chains.
-   Discussion: How do plants and animals depend on each other?

Day 2: Inquiry-Based Exploration

-   Guiding Questions:
-   What happens if one part of an ecosystem is removed?
-   How do plants and animals help each other?
-   Activity: Create a simple food chain using pictures and string.

Day 3: Interactive Lesson

-   Activity: Build a classroom ecosystem model using craft materials (e.g., shoeboxes, paper, plastic animals/plants).
-   Hands-On Activity: Students work in groups to create different ecosystem models (forest, ocean, desert, etc.).

Day 4: Metacognition Prompt

-   Prompt: "Think about the ecosystem model you created. How do the plants and animals in your model depend on each other? Write down your thoughts."

Day 5: Active Learning Experience

-   Activity: Present the ecosystem models to the class and explain the interdependence of the organisms within them.
-   Discussion: Reflect on how each student's model is unique and what they learned about ecosystems.

Culminating Authentic Performance Task

Objective: Students will demonstrate their understanding of living things by creating a project that showcases their knowledge of plants and animals.

Task: Create a Living Things Showcase

-   Description: Students will choose a living thing (plant or animal) and create a detailed project that includes:
-   A description of the living thing.
-   Its habitat.
-   Its life cycle.
-   How it interacts with other living things in its ecosystem.
-   Presentation: Students will present their projects to the class.

Rubric for Performance Task

Criteria	4 - Excellent	3 - Good	2 - Satisfactory	1 - Needs Improvement
Content Knowledge	Detailed and accurate information.	Accurate information with minor errors.	Basic information with some inaccuracies.	Incomplete and inaccurate information.
Creativity	Highly creative and original presentation.	Creative presentation with some originality.	Some creativity shown in presentation.	Lacks creativity; minimal effort shown.
Organization	Well-organized and easy to follow.	Organized with minor lapses in flow.	Some organization, but difficult to follow.	Disorganized and hard to follow.
Visuals	Excellent use of visuals; very engaging.	Good use of visuals; engaging.	Basic visuals; somewhat engaging.	Poor use of visuals; not engaging.
Presentation Skills	Clear, confident, and engaging speaking.	Clear and confident speaking.	Somewhat clear, but lacks confidence.	Unclear and lacks confidence.

Metacognitive Prompts throughout the Unit

- Week 1: "Think about the objects you classified. Why did you decide they were living or non-living? Write down your thoughts."
- Week 2: "Think about the plants you see every day. How do they grow and change? Write down your observations."
- Week 3: "Think about an animal you learned about this week. What makes it special? How is it different from other animals?"
- Week 4: "Think about the ecosystem model you created. How do the plants and animals in your model depend on each other? Write down your thoughts."

This unit design aims to make learning about living things relatable and exciting for second graders, fostering a classroom environment rich with curiosity and interaction.

Now, you can see in one lesson, GPT-4o suggests that students bring in living and non-living objects. Well, that would be completely nonsensical!

I also don't like the word "objective," so I would find and replace that word with "goal" if I was going to include this in curriculum documents.

> **@GPT-4o** *It would be ridiculous to ask students to bring in living and nonliving things. What would be another suggestion?*

Retrieved from GPT-4o https://poe.com/s/xgfmeO0nFGcLNrA83yEW, 2024

You're right; asking students to bring in living and non-living things can be impractical. Here's an alternative suggestion for a classroom-based activity that can achieve the same learning objectives:

Week 1: Introduction to Living Things

Objective: Students will understand the basic characteristics of living things and differentiate between living and non-living things.

Day 1: Engaging Introduction

- Activity: Watch an engaging video about living things (e.g., animals, plants).
- Discussion: What makes something alive? How can we tell the difference between living and non-living things?

Day 2: Characteristics of Living Things

- Interactive Lesson: Create a chart listing characteristics of living things (growth, reproduction, response to environment, etc.).

- Hands-On Activity: Use a collection of classroom objects (e.g., a rock, a paperclip, a plant, a stuffed animal) and images (e.g., pictures of animals, plants, the sun, a car). Students will classify these objects and images as living or non-living using a sorting activity.

Day 3: Inquiry-Based Exploration

- Guiding Questions:
- How do living things grow?
- What do living things need to survive?
- Activity: Plant seeds in small pots and predict what will happen.

Day 4: Metacognition Prompt

- Prompt: "Think about the objects you classified. Why did you decide they were living or non-living? Write down your thoughts."

Day 5: Active Learning Experience

- Activity: Nature walk to observe living and non-living things in the schoolyard.
- Discussion: Share observations and discuss the characteristics of the living things they saw.

Summary of Adjustments

Day 2 Hands-On Activity: Instead of bringing items from home, use classroom objects and printed images for the sorting activity. This ensures all students have access to the materials and keeps the activity manageable and safe.

This approach maintains the interactive and inquiry-based nature of the lesson while being practical and feasible for a classroom setting.

The project ideas and lesson experiences serve as invaluable springboards for educators. These outlines provide a foundation upon which teachers can build, adapt, and refine their own unique approaches to engaging students in the learning process. By offering a starting point, these ideas help educators avoid the daunting task of beginning with a blank page. Instead, they can draw inspiration from suggested activities, tweaking and tailoring them to fit the specific needs and interests of their students. This flexibility not only enriches the educational experience but also empowers teachers to innovate and personalize their instruction, ultimately leading to more meaningful and effective learning outcomes.

Example of Developing a Unit of Inquiry for Global Politics Grade12

> **Inquire**
>
> *Can you come up with a 12th-grade project-based learning unit on global politics?*
>
> **Design**
>
> *Outline the unit and include interactive inductive, inquiry-based lessons with an engaging intro to global politics: human rights, a hands-on activity for exploring. Include metacognition prompts and main activity learning experiences. Can you include guiding questions and give me four weeks' worth of inductive learning experiences and also include a culminating authentic performance task with a rubric in a table?*
>
> **Engage**
>
> *In this unit design, human rights need to be relatable and exciting for 12th graders, cultivating curiosity and interaction in the classroom.*

Retrieved from @GPT-4o-128k https://poe.com/s/ad6fBVDsfVInWsOedqSu, 2024

> 12th Grade Project-Based Learning Unit: Global Politics and Human Rights
>
> Unit Overview
>
> This four-week unit on global politics focuses on human rights. Students will engage in inquiry-based, interactive lessons designed to cultivate curiosity and foster deep understanding. They will explore human rights issues through hands-on activities, discussions, and research projects, culminating in an authentic performance task.
>
> Week 1: Introduction to Human Rights
>
> Engaging Intro Activity
> Title: "What Are Human Rights?"
>
> - Objective: Introduce students to the concept of human rights and their historical context.
> - Activity: Students watch a short documentary on the Universal Declaration of Human Rights (UDHR) followed by a class discussion.
> - Guiding Questions:
> - What are human rights?
> - How did the concept of human rights develop historically?
> - Why are human rights important in today's world?

Inquiry-Based Lesson

Title: "Human Rights in Our Lives"

- Objective: Connect human rights to students' personal experiences.
- Activity: Students create a "Human Rights Journal" where they document instances of human rights (or violations) they observe in their daily lives.
- Metacognition Prompt: Reflect on how understanding human rights changes your perspective on daily events.

Week 2: Case Studies in Human Rights

Interactive Lesson
Title: "Analyzing Human Rights Case Studies"

- Objective: Understand the application of human rights in different contexts.
- Activity: Students are divided into groups and assigned different human rights case studies (e.g., apartheid in South Africa, the Syrian refugee crisis, women's rights in Afghanistan). Each group presents their case study and discusses its impact.
- Guiding Questions:
- What human rights are being upheld or violated in this case?
- What are the social, political, and economic implications of these rights or violations?
- How do different stakeholders (governments, NGOs, individuals) respond to these issues?

Hands-On Activity
Title: "Human Rights Map"

- Objective: Visualize the global landscape of human rights.
- Activity: Groups create a digital or physical map highlighting different human rights issues around the world.
- Metacognition Prompt: Consider how geography and culture influence human rights issues.

Week 3: Human Rights and Global Politics

Inquiry-Based Lesson
Title: "Human Rights Organizations"

- Objective: Learn about organizations that work to protect human rights.
- Activity: Students research and present on various human rights organizations (e.g., Amnesty International, Human Rights Watch, UN Human Rights Council).

Guiding Questions:

- What are the main goals of these organizations?
- How do these organizations operate and influence global politics?
- What challenges do these organizations face?

Interactive Lesson
Title: "Simulating a UN Human Rights Council Meeting"

- Objective: Experience the complexities of global politics and human rights negotiations.
- Activity: Students role-play as representatives of different countries in a simulated UN Human Rights Council meeting, debating and negotiating resolutions on current human rights issues.
- Metacognition Prompt: Reflect on the challenges of reaching consensus on human rights issues in a global context.

Week 4: Culminating Authentic Performance Task

Performance Task
Title: "Human Rights Advocacy Campaign"

- Objective: Create a comprehensive campaign to raise awareness about a specific human rights issue.
- Activity: Students work in groups to develop an advocacy campaign, including a research report, a digital presentation, social media posts, and a plan for a community event.
- Guiding Questions:
- What human rights issue will your campaign focus on?
- Who is your target audience, and how will you engage them?
- What strategies will you use to raise awareness and advocate for change?

Rubric for Performance Task

Criteria	Excellent (4)	Good (3)	Satisfactory (2)	Needs Improvement (1)
Research Report	Thorough, well-organized, and insightful analysis	Clear and well-organized, with some insightful points	Adequate but lacks depth and organization	Lacks clarity, depth, and organization
Digital Presentation	Engaging, visually appealing, and informative	Clear and visually appealing with some engagement	Informative but not very engaging	Lacks clarity, visual appeal, and engagement
Social Media Posts	Creative, targeted, and impactful	Clear and targeted with some creativity	Adequate but lacks creativity and impact	Unclear, untargeted, and lacks creativity
Community Event Plan	Well-detailed, practical, and innovative	Practical and clear with some details	Adequate but lacks detail and innovation	Unclear, impractical, and lacks detail

Chapter Summary

This chapter explored into the art of crafting and refining prompts to enhance interactions with AI tools, emphasizing the dynamic, conversational nature of AI engagement rather than reliance on static prompt libraries. The chapter introduces the I.D.E.A.S. framework—Inquire, Design, Engage, Adapt, Synthesize—based on the five cannons of rhetoric— Inventio, Dispositio, Elocutio, Memoria, and Pronuntiatio—which further inform the art of communication when developing prompts. These principles from classical rhetoric are applied to modern AI interactions, illustrating how ancient communication strategies can enhance contemporary educational technologies.

I.D.E.A.S. is a structured yet adaptable method for developing effective prompts. Begin any interaction with an AI tool with inquire, design, and engage, and read the output before moving on to adapt and synthesize.

- **Inquire:** Begin by identifying what you want the AI tool to do. Clearly define the questions or tasks you want the AI to address.
- **Design:** Create specific prompts that guide the AI to design or generate the content you need. This step involves articulating your requirements in a way that the AI can understand and act upon.
- **Engage:** This includes deciding how it will present information to ensure an engaging learning experience.
- **Adapt and Synthesize:** Synthesize the information gathered through AI to enhance learning outcomes. Use the responses and feedback from the AI to refine your approach. Make necessary adjustments based on how well the AI's output meets your needs and enhances student engagement.

This approach helps in continuously refining the interactions to achieve clearer and more effective communication. By embracing this iterative approach, educators can surpass the limitations of mere prompt libraries to achieve the desired outcomes. The chapter concluded by highlighting the potential of well-crafted prompts to transform AI into a powerful tool for education, encouraging educators to embrace this dynamic process as part of their teaching strategy.

Discussion Questions

1. Reflecting on Prompt Libraries: The chapter suggested that relying solely on a prompt library can be cumbersome and limit creativity and flexibility. Discuss the advantages and disadvantages you've experienced using prompt libraries in your teaching. How can moving beyond these libraries enhance your interaction with any AI tool?

2. Importance of an Ongoing Natural Conversation: The chapter emphasized the value of treating interactions with AI as natural ongoing conversations. How does this approach change the way you might typically use AI tools? Share examples of how initiating a dynamic dialogue with AI could improve learning outcomes in your classes.

3. Applying the I.D.E.A.S. Framework: Discuss how the I.D.E.A.S. framework (Inquire, Design, Engage, Adapt, Synthesize) could be integrated into your interactions with any AI tool.

Artefact Opportunity

Prompt Development Workshop:

Try the I.D.E.A.S. framework, test the prompts with an AI tool, and iterate based on the responses. Share successful prompts and insights with the larger educational community.

CHAPTER 7
STREAMLINING SUCCESS

I imagine a world in which AI is going to make us work more
productively, live longer, and have cleaner energy.
—Fei-Fei Li

How Can AI Tools Enhance Educator Workflow and Creativity?

Artificial intelligence has been a fixture for some time now, and while I may be relatively new to its applications, my journey with it began with just three interactions with ChatGPT. I decided to delve deeper, and I was struck by the vast array of AI educational tools available, which, while impressive, can also feel daunting. I came to understand throughout my exploration of AI the importance of possessing a thorough understanding of how to incorporate it effectively into teaching pedagogy and apply it in an appropriate way.

As an educator, I currently use a range of AI tools. These tools have significantly enhanced my productivity and served as invaluable springboards for ideas for lesson planning. With a single prompt I can generate loads of ideas for a lesson or unit that I can then adapt to fit what I need. Additionally, I use AI to generate marking rubrics, with the practice of cross-referencing the prompts across different tools to find what best suits my students and teaching environment. I would caution anyone to also use additional prompts in order to achieve the best result.

As with any AI tool, it is important to recognize that you must make adaptations to align with your needs, alongside an understanding of AI's inherent limitations. There are so many uses for teachers to help save time, but I think you need to beware that these tools aren't infallible.

It has been essential to approach the use of AI with a critical eye. Understanding the ethical implications and weighing the pros and cons are imperative for responsible integration into teaching practices.

Angela Skinner, New Zealand teacher, grade 3 teacher, Qatar Academy Al Wakra

Teachers are constantly crunched for time—it's a universal struggle! This chapter explores how AI can be a game-changer for planning and workflow—saving us all time! We'll focus on how AI can supercharge your efficiency, all while ensuring you stay in the driver's seat. You'll remain in control of your content and empowered to make choices based on the insights AI tools provide.

Enhancing Educator Workflow

It's no secret: teachers are juggling more than ever before. But imagine a world where AI steps in to handle the routine, freeing you to focus on what truly matters: connecting with your students and fostering their growth. AI can be that helping hand, streamlining your workflow so you can pour your energy into creating a vibrant and engaging learning environment.

AI offer powerful tools to streamline workflows and alleviate the burden of mundane tasks, allowing educators to focus on what truly matters: building relationships and student learning and engagement. By automating routine administrative tasks, and providing instant feedback, AI can enhance efficiency and effectiveness, empowering educators to create a more dynamic and impactful learning environment. Here are some of the ways AI can enhance teachers' workflow.

1. Administrative Task Automation

AI technology offers transformative potential in streamlining various administrative and routine tasks that often consume a significant portion of teachers' time. By leveraging AI, educators can automate grading, manage scheduling, and handle communications more efficiently, freeing up time to focus on student interactions and encouraging a better work-life balance. The integration of AI not only enhances productivity but also improves the overall educational experience by allowing teachers to dedicate more energy to their primary mission: fostering student learning and growth.

Image generated by DALL·E 3, 2024

- Scheduling and Reminders: AI assistants can schedule meetings, set reminders for important deadlines, and coordinate parent-teacher conferences.
- Routine Administrative Tasks: AI can handle various routine administrative tasks such as attendance tracking and communication with parents. This reduces the administrative burden on teachers, freeing up more time for instructional planning and student interaction.

- School Timetabling: AI is revolutionizing the creation of school timetables by efficiently managing the complex web of constraints that often complicate scheduling. These constraints can include teacher availability, room assignments, class sizes, and specific student needs. Advanced AI algorithms can analyze vast amounts of data to optimize schedules, ensuring all requirements are met while minimizing conflicts. This not only saves administrators time but also creates more balanced and effective timetables, enhancing the overall educational experience for both students and staff.

Example Tools: ClassDojo, PowerSchool, MagicSchool

By handling routine administrative tasks such as scheduling, AI tools significantly alleviate the time burden on educators. This automation enables teachers to maintain effective and streamlined scheduling without the associated stress, ultimately allowing them to dedicate more energy to their core responsibilities of teaching and student engagement.

2. Parent-Teacher Communication

- Description: AI can facilitate better communication between parents and teachers by drafting emails, automating routine updates, scheduling parent-teacher conferences, and providing insights into student progress and behavior.

  Example Tools: ParentSquare, MagicSchool

Managing email communication can be time-consuming for teachers, especially when dealing with frequent inquiries from students and parents. AI can help simplify and streamline this process by drafting and sending routine emails such as reminders, announcements, and follow-ups, saving teachers considerable time.

3. AI Chatbots

- **Specific AI Chatbots:** AI chatbots can be tailored to meet the specific needs of different departments within your school. For instance, the HR department could deploy an AI chatbot to answer basic questions about contracts, benefits, and other human resources-related inquiries. This would streamline communication and free up HR staff to focus on more complex issues. Similarly, the Math department could utilize an AI chatbot to address questions about the syllabus, guide students through assessments, and provide additional resources for learning specific mathematical concepts. This helps ensure that students and parents receive timely and accurate information, enhancing the educational experience.

- **Instant Feedback on Assignments:** AI chatbots can provide instant feedback on assignments, helping students improve their work in real-time. Tools such as Grammarly, Quill, and ProWritingAid can analyze writing, suggest corrections, and offer tips for enhancement.
- **Language Practice:** AI chatbots can engage in conversations in the target language, assisting students with language practice. This interactive approach helps students develop their language skills through practical, conversational experiences.

By integrating AI chatbots into the community and learning process, schools can streamline certain processes and teachers can enhance student engagement, provide immediate feedback, and support language development. This not only enriches the educational experience but also allows teachers to focus more on personalized instruction and other critical teaching activities.

4. Real-Time Language Translation and Accessibility Tools

- **Real-Time Language Translation:** For classrooms with non-native speakers, AI-powered tools can provide real-time language translation. This ensures that all students can understand and engage with the material equally.
- **Accessibility Features:** AI tools offering speech-to-text or text-to-speech services (and soon speech-to-speech) can help neurodiverse students access and interact with classroom content more effectively, creating a more inclusive learning environment.

- **Translanguaging Support:** Another crucial aspect of these tools is translanguaging, which acknowledges and leverages students' full linguistic repertoires. Translanguaging allows students to use their home languages alongside the language of instruction, fostering a deeper understanding and more meaningful learning experiences.

By integrating AI tools that support efficient translations, educators can facilitate seamless transitions between languages, enhance comprehension, and validate the linguistic and cultural identities of all students. This not only aids in language development but also ensures that every student has the opportunity to participate fully and confidently in classroom activities.

5. Student Recommendation Letters

- **Personalized Reference Letters:** AI can help generate personalized student reference letters by analyzing student data and performance. This provides a solid draft that teachers can then refine, saving time and ensuring that each letter highlights the student's strengths and achievements effectively.
- By leveraging AI for this task, educators can generate a high-quality skeleton draft of a recommendation letter, saving valuable time. This allows them to quickly refine and personalize the content, without being bogged down by the initial drafting process.

By leveraging AI for this task, educators can generate a high-quality skeleton draft of a recommendation letter, saving valuable time. This allows them to quickly refine and personalize the content, without being bogged down by the initial drafting process.

6. AI-Driven Data Visualization

- **Description:** AI tools can transform complex data into easy-to-understand visualizations, helping educators analyze student performance, track progress, and identify trends. This enables educators to make data-driven decisions and tailor their teaching strategies accordingly.

Example Tools: Tableau, GPT-4o, Google Data Studio (Looker Studio)

These are just a few examples of how AI can enhance workflow and save time for educators. By automating routine tasks, generating draft documents, and providing real-time feedback, AI empowers teachers to focus more on what truly matters—engaging with students and fostering a dynamic learning environment. There are many more ways AI can be integrated into educational practices to improve efficiency and effectiveness, offering endless possibilities for innovation in the classroom.

Boosting Educator Creativity

AI tools hold immense potential to spark creativity in educators, offering innovative avenues for student engagement and enriching learning experiences. By embracing AI, teachers can explore new horizons in content creation, design dynamic interactive activities, and develop lessons with greater impact. This section delves into how AI can empower educators to break free from traditional teaching methods and infuse their practices with fresh, imaginative approaches.

1. Enhancing Curriculum Planning:

- **Brainstorming:** AI can facilitate brainstorming sessions by generating creative ideas for any aspect of curriculum planning.
- **Lesson Plan Suggestions:** AI can provide innovative lesson plan ideas and templates aligned with curriculum standards, saving time on planning and increasing teaching effectiveness.
- **Project Creation and Management:** AI can also assist teachers in creating engaging and educational for curriculum projects and managing them more effectively. AI tools can suggest project ideas, provide templates, and offer step-by-step guides to help educators design innovative and interactive projects that align with curriculum standards.
- **Resource Recommendations:** AI can curate and recommend educational resources such as articles, videos, and interactive tools (see the "Create with AI tool" on Padlet) that align with specific lessons or units.

    Example Tools: PowerSchool, MagicSchool, Eduaide, Padlet, any LLM

AI can significantly enrich the curriculum planning process by providing a plethora of creative ideas and suggestions that align with the best pedagogical practices. AI can offer innovative ideas and teaching strategies, helping educators design lessons that are both engaging and educationally sound. This approach allows for meaningful curriculum development, ensuring that lesson plans remain relevant, and adaptable to various learning environments, thereby enhancing the overall educational experience.

2. Content Creation and Enhancement

- **Multimedia Content Creation:** AI can aid in creating multimedia content, such as interactive videos, quizzes, and presentations. Tools like Canva and Adobe Spark use AI to simplify the design process, enabling teachers to create visually appealing materials without extensive graphic design skills.

  Example Tools: Canva, Adobe Spark, Curipod

By utilizing AI for content creation, educators can produce engaging and high-quality materials efficiently, enhancing the overall learning experience for their students.

3. Creative Writing and Storytelling Assistance

- **Writing Prompts and Story Development:** AI tools can assist in creative writing and storytelling by providing prompts, character development suggestions, and plot ideas. These tools can analyze themes, genres, and writing styles to generate ideas that align with the lesson objectives. Educators can use these AI-generated elements to design more engaging and creative writing assignments or storytelling sessions, encouraging students to explore their imagination and improve their writing skills.

4. Interactive Simulations and Lab Experiments

- **Virtual Lab Experiences:** AI can create interactive simulations and virtual lab experiments, allowing students to explore complex concepts in a controlled, risk-free environment. These simulations can mimic real-world processes and experiments, providing hands-on learning experiences without the constraints of physical resources. This can inspire educators to incorporate more experiential learning activities into their curriculum, making subjects like science and engineering more accessible and engaging.

Example Tool: PhET Interactive Simulations: Offers free, simulations in science and math, allowing students to manipulate variables and observe outcomes in real-time. Although these are technically not AI tools, they do use AI to create the simulations.

5. AI-Powered Art and Music Creation

- **Art and Music Generation:** AI can assist in the creation of art and music by generating artwork or composing music based on specific inputs from educators. These tools can analyze styles, themes, and genres to produce original pieces that can be used in classroom projects or activities. This can be a great tool for art, music, or any teachers looking to inspire creativity in their students, as it allows them to explore different artistic expressions and musical compositions without needing extensive technical skills.

Example Tools: DALL·E 3, Shutterstock AI Image Generator, Mubert, MagicSchool

Chapter Summary

In this chapter, we discussed into the crucial role that educators play in integrating AI into their planning and workflow. We focus on how AI can enhance workflow efficiency and amplify instructional capabilities while ensuring that educators remain in control of the educational content and make informed decisions based on AI outputs. AI tools can automate routine administrative tasks such as scheduling, attendance tracking, and communication with parents, significantly reducing the administrative burden on teachers. This automation allows educators to dedicate more time to instructional planning and student engagement, ultimately enhancing the learning experience.

Additionally, AI can streamline parent-teacher communication, provide instant feedback on student assignments, and offer real-time language translation and accessibility features to create a more inclusive learning environment. AI can also assist in generating personalized drafts of student recommendation letters, saving valuable time for educators. These examples illustrate how AI can support educators in focusing on what truly matters—engaging with students and fostering a dynamic learning environment.

This chapter also explored how AI can boost educator creativity. AI tools present unique opportunities to enhance and inspire creativity, offering innovative ways to engage students and enrich their learning experiences. By integrating AI, teachers can explore new methods of content creation, facilitate dynamic interactive activities, and develop more impactful lessons. AI can assist in curriculum planning by providing lesson plan suggestions, project ideas, and resource recommendations, and aid in creating multimedia content and interactive simulations.

By leveraging AI, educators can move beyond traditional methods and introduce fresh, imaginative approaches into their teaching practices, ultimately fostering a more engaging and exciting educational environment.

Discussion Questions

1. How can AI tools specifically help you in automating routine administrative tasks in your daily teaching practice? Discuss how AI can reduce the time spent on administrative tasks such as scheduling, attendance tracking, and parent communication. What specific tasks do you find most time-consuming, and how could AI alleviate this burden?

2. In what ways can AI enhance communication between teachers, parents, and students? Explore the potential of AI to streamline and improve communication channels. How might AI tools like chatbots and automated emails change the way you interact with parents and students? What benefits and challenges do you foresee?

3. What are some innovative ways you can incorporate AI to boost creativity in your curriculum planning and teaching practices? Reflect on how AI can assist in generating lesson plan ideas, creating multimedia content, and developing interactive simulations. How can these tools inspire you to try new teaching methods and enhance student engagement?

Artefact Opportunity

AI Tool Exploration:

Choose an AI tool that can help streamline your workflow (e.g., scheduling, grading). Experiment with the tool, document the experience, and share how it affected workflow and efficiency with your colleagues.

PART 3

LEARNER-CENTRIC AI USE: ENHANCING HUMANITY

HOW CAN AI-POWERED PEDAGOGY DEVELOP THE ETHICAL AND HUMANISTIC LEARNER?

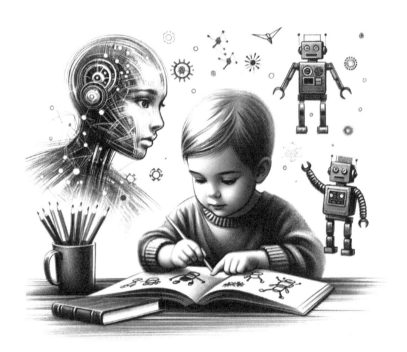

Image generated by DALL·E 3, 2024

CHAPTER 8
THE ETHICAL LEARNER

*If you were a computer and read all the AI articles and extracted out the
names that are quoted, I guarantee you that women rarely show up.
For every woman who has been quoted about AI technology,
there are a hundred more times men were quoted.*
—Fei-Fei Li, computer scientist at Stanford University

How Might We Develop Ethical Learners?

I recently tasked my master's students with a challenge: analyze a dense, lengthy document using an AI tool designed for rapid information synthesis. While some groups expertly navigated this task, confirming the AI's output against the original text, one group stumbled. They presented findings that were demonstrably incorrect, placing the blame squarely on the AI. "It just got it wrong," they insisted. This raised a red flag. It's perplexing why they didn't engage in critical evaluation, especially knowing that AI can sometimes generate factually incorrect information. Why did they share the output of an AI tool without revising? This situation unveiled a concerning gap in their AI literacy, pointing toward a larger ethical dilemma. Are we equipping students with powerful AI tools without instilling the critical thinking skills and ethical awareness necessary to wield them responsibly? The implications are significant, urging us to consider the kind of digital citizens we are shaping in an increasingly AI-driven world.

As AI becomes increasingly integrated into our lives, it's vital to address the ethical considerations that accompany its use. This chapter explores how we can teach students to use AI responsibly and ethically. We'll examine the importance of recognizing bias, understanding ethical frameworks, and challenging stereotypes in AI applications. Our aim is to cultivate a new generation of digital citizens who are not only adept at using AI but also deeply aware of its ethical implications.

Image generated by DALL·E 3 2024

Ethical use of AI is about ensuring that our use of this powerful tool is always fair and just, avoiding biases that could harm or marginalize some students. By empowering users, and I mean giving both learners and educators the tools and knowledge they need to use AI effectively and responsibly, we can ensure that technology serves us, not the other way around. So, you see, it's about guiding AI development in ways that not only enhance educational outcomes but also align with our deepest values as educators.

Understanding Ethics

Ethics encompasses the principles and guidelines that govern the development and deployment of AI. As AI systems increasingly influence various aspects of life, from healthcare to criminal justice, it becomes paramount to instill ethical and responsible use.

Teaching students about AI ethics involves the following:

1. **Moral Responsibility:** Emphasizing the moral responsibilities of those who develop and use AI systems. Students should understand that their choices can impact society positively or negatively.

2. **Transparency and Accountability:** Advocating for transparency in AI processes and accountability for the outcomes produced by AI systems. This ensures that AI operations are understandable and that there is a clear chain of responsibility.

3. **Privacy and Security:** Educating students about the importance of data privacy and the measures needed to protect personal information from misuse or unauthorized access.

Educators play a pivotal role in instilling ethical values through meaningful learning experiences and by examining case studies. The following are some examples of ethics lessons generated by AI from an IB theory of knowledge teacher. Here is an exciting account from a very experienced teacher on one example of AI used in TOK lessons generated on Poe's Llama-3-70B-T (May 3, 2024):

> I have been playing around with AI for a while and have been working on refining the quality of my prompts:
>
> In a high school theory of knowledge class, with bated breath, students gathered as I unveiled the AI-weaved vivid scenarios, describing intricate human science experiments. Each of them was designed to discuss ethics, one of the four cornerstones of the TOK framework.
>
> After providing their consent in taking part, students formed groups, each assigned a unique AI-generated human science experiment to test their sense of cultural bias. Immersed in lively discussions, they delved deep into the ethical implications, dissecting the potential risks, benefits, and moral dilemmas surrounding each scenario.

Animated debates ensued as students grappled with the ethical intricacies, considering the psychological impact on participants and the importance of informed consent. With minds ablaze, they applied TOK concepts to critically analyze the experiments' reliability, validity, and ethical implications. The classroom became an intellectual battleground of ideas, fostering empathy, critical thinking, and an appreciation for the ethical challenges embedded within the realm of human sciences. Empowered with newfound knowledge, the students emerged as conscientious thinkers, equipped to navigate the ethical complexities that underpin knowledge production in the human sciences.

Here are the scenarios we used:

Experiment 1: "The Cultural Lens"

Setup: A diverse group of students is presented with a series of images depicting various cultural practices, traditions, and customs from around the world. Each student is given a pair of glasses with a unique cultural lens (e.g., Western, Eastern, African, etc.) that influences their perception of the images.

Methodology: Students are asked to describe and interpret the images while wearing their assigned cultural lens. They then discuss their observations in small groups, exploring how their cultural bias affects their understanding of the images.

Findings: This experiment reveals how cultural bias can shape our perceptions and interpretations of cultural practices, highlighting the importance of considering multiple perspectives in knowledge production.

Experiment 2: "The Blinded Interview"

Setup: Students are paired up for a mock job interview, with one student acting as the interviewer and the other as the interviewee. The twist: the interviewer is given a set of biased assumptions about the interviewee's cultural background, while the interviewee remains unaware of these assumptions.

Methodology: The interview proceeds as usual, with the interviewer asking questions and making notes. After the interview, the students discuss their experiences, exploring how the biased assumptions influenced the interview process.

Findings: This experiment demonstrates how cultural bias can affect our interactions and decision-making processes, often unconsciously. It highlights the importance of recognizing and addressing these biases in professional and personal settings.

Experiment 3: "The Cultural Mashup"

Setup: Students are divided into small groups and tasked with creating a new cultural practice or tradition by combining elements from different cultures. They are given a set of random cultural artifacts, music, and images to inspire their creation.

Methodology: Each group presents their cultural mashup, explaining the cultural influences and significance behind their creation. The class then discusses the implications of cultural fusion, exploring how it can both enrich and challenge our understanding of cultural identity.

Findings: This experiment reveals the complexities of cultural exchange and the potential for cultural bias to influence our perceptions of cultural fusion. It highlights the importance of considering the ethical implications of cultural appropriation and appreciation.

Experiment 4: "The Cultural Artifact Challenge"

Methodology: Students are divided into groups and asked to bring in a cultural artifact that represents their own cultural background. The artifacts are anonymously displayed, and each group is given the task of analyzing and interpreting the artifacts from a neutral perspective. They must identify any potential biases or assumptions they may have and critically evaluate how these biases influence their understanding of the artifacts.

Ethical Justification: This experiment aims to raise awareness of cultural biases by encouraging students to reflect on their own perspectives. It fosters an appreciation for the diversity of cultural expressions while promoting empathy and understanding. The anonymity of the artifacts mitigates any potential harm or prejudice that could arise from personal judgments.

Generated by Llama-3-70B-T, 2024
Lucie Lecocq-Otsing
French / TOK DP teacher / IBDP coordinator and curriculum leader

Deepfakes

In 2023, Academy Award-winning actor Tom Hanks took to Instagram to express his concerns about the unauthorized use of AI to recreate his likeness, highlighting a deepfake video featuring an AI-generated version of himself promoting a dental plan. Hanks's warning brought to light the growing issue of deepfakes and the ethical dilemmas surrounding the use of AI to manipulate and exploit the images of public figures without their consent. Deepfakes, hyper-realistic digital alterations created using AI, can generate convincing yet entirely fabricated images, videos, or audio recordings capable of deceiving the public, manipulating opinions, and damaging reputations. Infamous examples include fabricated videos of former U.S. president Barack Obama and Facebook CEO Mark Zuckerberg, demonstrating the potential for deepfakes to spread misinformation and undermine trust in public figures and institutions.

The potential for misuse of AI, particularly in creating unauthorized digital replicas, was a driving force behind the recent 100-day actors' strike in Hollywood. The Screen Actors Guild-American Federation of Television and Radio Artists (SAG-AFTRA) demanded protections to prevent studios from creating digital replicas or AI-generated likenesses of actors without their explicit consent and additional compensation. Actors feared that studios could use AI to generate synthetic performances or digitally manipulate their images and voices, potentially replacing them in future projects without their involvement.

Understanding deepfakes and their ethical implications is crucial in today's digital age. Here are some practical applications and strategies for teaching learners about deepfakes and their ethical issues from GPT-4o-128K:

1. Interactive Workshops and Seminars

- Activity: Host workshops where students learn how deepfakes are created and how they can be detected.
- Objective: Provide hands-on experience with AI tools to create simple deepfakes, followed by sessions on identifying and debunking them.
- Discussion: Facilitate discussions on the ethical ramifications of using such technology, focusing on privacy, consent, and misinformation.

2. Case Study Analysis

- Activity: Analyze famous cases of deepfakes, such as the Obama and Zuckerberg videos, and the actors' strike regarding AI use in the entertainment industry.
- Objective: Encourage critical thinking about the impact of deepfakes on public trust, personal privacy, and societal norms.
- Discussion: Explore the ethical dilemmas faced by those who create, distribute, or fall victim to deepfakes.

3. Debate and Role-Playing

- Activity: Organize debates where students take on roles of different stakeholders, such as AI developers, government regulators, and individuals affected by deepfakes.
- Objective: Develop empathy and understanding of multiple perspectives on the ethical use of AI technology.
- Discussion: Debate the balance between innovation and regulation, and the responsibilities of creators and users of AI technologies.

4. Digital Literacy Curriculum Integration

- Activity: Integrate lessons on digital literacy that include units on identifying and understanding deepfakes.
- Objective: Equip students with the skills to critically evaluate digital content and recognize manipulated media.
- Discussion: Teach students about the broader implications of deepfakes on society, politics, and personal relationships.

5. Ethics in Technology Projects

- Activity: Assign projects where students must research and present on the ethical use of AI and deepfakes in various fields, such as journalism, entertainment, and law.
- Objective: Foster deep research skills and ethical reasoning by examining real-world applications and consequences.
- Discussion: Encourage students to propose guidelines or policies for the ethical use of AI in creating digital content.

6. Guest Speakers and Expert Panels

- Activity: Invite experts in AI, digital forensics, and ethics to speak to students or participate in panel discussions.
- Objective: Provide students with professional insights and real-world perspectives on the challenges and ethical considerations of deepfakes.
- Discussion: Allow students to ask questions and engage with professionals, deepening their understanding of the subject matter.

7. Simulation of Real-World Scenarios

- Activity: Create simulations where students must address a crisis involving a deep fake, such as a fake news scenario or a compromised celebrity image.
- Objective: Develop problem-solving and crisis-management skills in a controlled educational setting.
- Discussion: Reflect on the steps taken during the simulation, the ethical decisions made, and the outcomes achieved.

8. Creating Awareness Campaigns

- Activity: Task students with designing awareness campaigns to educate the public about deepfakes and their ethical implications.
- Objective: Promote civic engagement and the responsible use of technology.
- Discussion: Evaluate the effectiveness of different campaign strategies and the importance of public awareness in combating misinformation.

By implementing these practical applications, educators can help students understand the complexities and ethical issues surrounding deepfakes, preparing them to navigate and influence the digital world responsibly.

Understanding Bias in AI Tools

Many teachers I work with are surprised to discover that AI systems can perpetuate and even amplify biases present in their training data. This inherent bias, often not noticeable at first glance, highlights the critical need for careful examination and mitigation strategies when implementing AI in educational settings.

> Cultural bias in AI is the same as in people. The information that we take in creates our bias. We are all a sum of the experiences we have had, the things we have read and been told. Our bias is a function of that input. It is the same for AI, particularly LLMs.
>
> **Chris Binge**
> **International Educator**

Recognizing and Countering Bias

AI systems can inadvertently perpetuate biases because they learn patterns and make decisions based on the information they are fed, which may reflect existing societal prejudices or historical inequities. This can lead to unfair or prejudiced outcomes. Here are a few types of the biases AI tools can perpetuate:

1. **Algorithmic Bias:** The algorithms and machine learning techniques used to build the AI system can exhibit biases, such as favoring certain outcomes or features over others. E.g. An AI-based credit scoring system that disproportionately assigns lower credit scores to women because it overemphasizes certain financial behaviors more common among men, leading to gender-based discrepancies in creditworthiness assessments.

2. **Confirmation Bias:** When individuals favor information that confirms their pre-existing beliefs or values. While this is a cognitive bias, it can influence the design and interpretation of AI systems if the developers or users are not objective. E.g. A social media platform's recommendation algorithm that suggests content similar to what

users have previously engaged with. This can lead to echo chambers where users are only exposed to viewpoints that confirm their pre-existing beliefs, reinforcing those beliefs over time.

3. **Training Data Bias:** AI systems learn from vast amounts of data, making it crucial to ensure this data is free from bias. Training data bias can manifest in several ways, including sampling bias, where certain groups are over-represented or under-represented, leading to skewed outcomes. For example, a facial recognition system trained primarily on images of white people may struggle to accurately identify people of color. Another form of bias is labeling bias, where the way data is labeled can introduce unfair preferences or exclusions. For instance, AI recruiting tools that use inconsistent labeling or exclude certain characteristics could unfairly eliminate qualified candidates. Addressing these biases is essential to creating fair and equitable AI systems.

4. **Measurement Bias:** Occurs when the data collected for training an AI system is systematically distorted or inaccurate. This can happen due to errors in data collection methods or instrumentation, for example, a health-monitoring AI that uses a specific type of wearable device to collect data. If the device consistently underestimates heart rates during physical activity due to poor sensor placement, the AI's predictions about users' fitness levels will be inaccurate.

5. **Aggregation Bias:** When data from different sources or groups is combined in a way that masks important differences or nuances, leading to biased conclusions. For example, a healthcare AI that aggregates patient data from various countries without adjusting for regional dietary habits and environmental factors may produce inaccurate diagnostic predictions and treatment recommendations.

6. **Historical Bias:** When the data reflects historical inequities or social prejudices, perpetuating and reinforcing these biases in AI outcomes, for example, a loan-approval AI trained on historical lending data

that includes discriminatory practices against minority groups. The AI might continue to deny loans to these groups at higher rates, reflecting and perpetuating past inequities.

Strategies for Mitigating Bias in AI Tools

Figure 8.1 below highlights essential strategies for ensuring fairness in the use of AI tools. It emphasizes the importance of diversifying data sets to create more representative AI, maintaining human oversight to detect and address bias, encouraging students to think critically about AI and its limitations, offering alternative options for students who feel an AI tool is biased, and reporting instances of bias to developers to improve the tool's fairness.

Figure 8.1:

How to Mitigate Bias

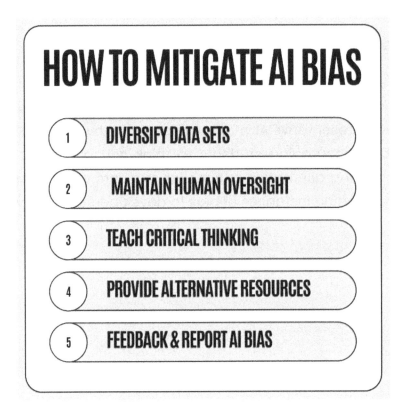

Facilitating classroom conversations about biases in AI helps students engage critically with these issues. Additionally, analyzing real-world scenarios where AI biases are in question encourages students to propose and debate solutions, fostering a deeper understanding of the ethical implications and responsibilities associated with AI technology.

Another effective approach is to conduct bias-detection exercises where students actively examine AI outputs using carefully selected tools or datasets that demonstrate how skewed inputs can lead to biased interpretations by the AI system. Through these hands-on activities, students gain a deeper understanding of the potential pitfalls and learn strategies to mitigate biases in AI applications.

Teaching Learners about Ethical and Biases in the AI World

Developing students' ability to make ethical decisions in the use of AI is crucial. This involves understanding the implications of their choices when interacting with or deploying AI technologies:

- **Ethical Frameworks:** Introduce students to ethical frameworks and principles that guide decision-making in AI, such as the Asilomar AI Principles.
- **Simulation-Based Learning:** Use simulations to allow students to experience the consequences of ethical and unethical AI use in controlled, reflective learning environments.

The aim of this section is to equip learners with the knowledge and critical thinking skills necessary to navigate and influence the evolving AI landscape responsibly.

Examples of Lessons on AI Ethics from GPT-4-128K

Examples of Ethical Frameworks

Example 1: Introducing the Asilomar AI Principles

Familiarize students with ethical guidelines for AI development and use.

Activity:

1. Introduction to Principles: Explain the Asilomar AI Principles, which include guidelines on transparency, safety, and fairness in AI.
2. Case Study Analysis: Present students with real-world case studies where AI ethics were in question (e.g., bias in facial recognition software).
3. Discussion: Students discuss how the Asilomar AI Principles could be applied to each case study.

Discussion Questions:

- How do the Asilomar AI Principles help in addressing ethical issues in the case studies?
- Can you think of any additional principles that should be included to cover emerging ethical concerns?

Example 2: Ethics in AI Development

Help students develop their own ethical guidelines for AI projects.

Activity:

1. Group Work: Divide students into small groups and ask them to develop a set of ethical guidelines for a hypothetical AI project (e.g., an AI for hiring employees).
2. Presentation: Each group presents their guidelines and explains the reasoning behind them.
3. Peer Review: Groups critique each other's guidelines, providing constructive feedback based on established ethical frameworks.

Discussion Questions:

- What challenges did you face while developing the ethical guidelines?
- How did existing ethical frameworks influence your decisions?

Simulation-Based Learning

Example 1: AI in Healthcare Simulation

Simulate ethical decision-making in the deployment of AI in a healthcare setting.

Simulation:

1. Scenario Setup: Create a scenario where an AI system is used to prioritize patients for surgery based on various factors (e.g., age, medical history, urgency).
2. Roles: Assign students roles such as doctors, patients, AI developers, and ethics committee members.
3. Decision-Making: Students must decide how to use the AI system ethically. They must consider the implications of their choices on patient outcomes and fairness.

Debrief Questions:

- What ethical dilemmas did you encounter during the simulation?
- How did your decisions align with ethical principles like fairness and transparency?

Example 2: AI in Hiring Simulation

Understand the ethical implications of using AI in hiring processes.

Simulation:

1. Scenario Setup: Create a scenario where an AI system is used to screen job applicants. The AI has been found to have biases against certain demographics.

2. Roles: Assign students roles such as hiring managers, job applicants, AI developers, and diversity officers.
3. Decision-Making: Students must decide how to address the biases in the AI system and ensure a fair hiring process.

Debrief Questions:

- What steps did you take to identify and mitigate biases in the AI system?
- How did your decisions impact the fairness and inclusivity of the hiring process?

These examples provide practical ways to teach ethical decision-making in AI use. By introducing students to ethical frameworks and engaging them in simulation-based learning, educators can help students understand the implications of their choices and develop the skills needed to navigate the complex ethical landscape of AI technology.

Culminating Project: Ethical AI Design Challenge

As a practical application of the concepts discussed, students will participate in an "Ethical AI Design Challenge." They will:

- **Design an AI Solution:** Work in groups to design an AI solution for a given problem, ensuring their approach adheres to ethical standards discussed in the class.
- **Present and Critique:** Present their AI designs to peers, who will critique based on ethical considerations, fostering a deeper understanding and application of ethical AI use.

Example 1: Privacy and Data Collection

Scenario: Discuss with students how a smart assistant (like Siri or Alexa) collects data to help answer questions or play music.

Discussion Questions:

- How does the smart assistant know what music you like?
- What kind of information do you think it collects to answer your questions?
- Why is it important to keep some information private?

Example 2: Autonomous Vehicles

Scenario: Discuss the concept of self-driving cars and how they make decisions on the road.

Discussion Questions:

- What should a self-driving car do if it has to choose between hitting a tree or another car?
- How can we teach the car to make safe decisions?
- Why is it important for the car to follow traffic rules?

Image generated by DALL·E 3, 2024

Recognizing and Countering Bias

Bias Detection Exercises

Exercise 1: Image Classification Bias

Goal: Identify biases in an AI system trained to classify images.

Materials Needed: A dataset with diverse images, an AI image classifier, and a whiteboard.

Steps:

1. Show students how the AI classifies different images.
2. Ask students to note any patterns or biases (e.g., misclassifying images of people with darker skin tones).
3. Discuss why these biases might exist and how they could impact real-world applications.

Can you draw a black-and-white sketch of a Chinese person?

Image created by StableDiffusionXL 2024

Discussion Questions:

- Why do you think the AI misclassified certain images?
- How can we improve the training data to reduce these biases?

Exercise 2: Gender Bias in Job Descriptions

Detect gender bias in AI-generated job descriptions.

Materials Needed: Several AI-generated job descriptions and markers.

Steps:

1. Provide students with various job descriptions.
2. Ask them to highlight words or phrases that might be biased toward a particular gender.
3. Discuss how these biases could affect job applicants.

Can you draw a black-and-white sketch of a mathematics teacher?

Image generated by DALL·E 3,

Discussion Questions:

- How could biased language in job descriptions discourage certain applicants?
- What changes can we make to ensure job descriptions are more inclusive?

Role-Playing Scenarios

Scenario 1: Doctor and AI Diagnosis System

Understand the implications of biased AI in healthcare.

Roles: Doctor, Patient, AI System.

Scenario: The AI system suggests a diagnosis based on biased training data.

Steps:

1. The "Patient" describes their symptoms to the "Doctor."
2. The "Doctor" receives a diagnosis suggestion from the "AI System."
3. The "Doctor" must decide whether to follow the AI's suggestion or use their own judgment.

Discussion Questions:

-   How should the doctor approach the AI's suggestion if they suspect bias?
-   What are the potential consequences of relying solely on the AI's diagnosis?

Scenario 2: Hiring Manager and AI Recruitment Tool

Explore biases in AI-assisted hiring processes.

Roles: hiring manager, job applicant, AI recruitment tool

Scenario: The AI tool prioritizes candidates based on biased criteria.

Steps:

1. The "job applicant" submits their resume.
2. The "AI recruitment tool" scores the applicant based on biased criteria (e.g., favoring certain schools).
3. The "hiring manager" reviews the AI's recommendation and decides whether to interview the applicant.

Discussion Questions:

-   How can the hiring manager identify potential biases in the AI's recommendations?
-   What steps can be taken to ensure a fair hiring process?

Scenario 3: Judge and AI Legal Advisor

Understand the impact of biased AI in the judicial system.

Roles: judge, defendant, AI legal advisor

Scenario: The AI legal advisor suggests a sentence based on biased data.

Steps:

1. The "defendant" presents their case.
2. The "AI legal advisor" offers a sentencing recommendation.
3. The "judge" must decide whether to follow the AI's suggestion or consider other factors.

Discussion Questions:

- How can the judge ensure that the AI's recommendation is fair and unbiased?
- What are the risks of relying too heavily on AI in the judicial system?

These learning experiences and role-playing scenarios help learners recognize and counteract different types of biases in AI systems. By engaging in these activities, students can develop a deeper understanding of the ethical challenges associated with AI and learn strategies to promote fairness and inclusivity.

Using AI to Challenge Stereotypes

While AI can inadvertently perpetuate existing societal stereotypes, it also presents an opportunity to challenge them and broaden student perspectives. Educators can leverage AI-assisted content creation to encourage students to develop projects reflecting diverse cultures and viewpoints, directly confronting prevailing stereotypes.

Further, incorporating critical media literacy into the curriculum empowers students to critically assess AI-generated media, enabling them to identify and question stereotypical representations. Through these methods, AI can become a powerful force for promoting inclusivity and challenging harmful stereotypes.

Here are some examples of lessons that incorporate AI-assisted content creation from GPT-4-128k:

Example 1: Diverse Storytelling Grades Pre-K–12

Use AI to help students create stories that reflect diverse cultures and viewpoints.

Activity:

1. AI Tool: Utilize an AI-powered story generator using any LLM.
2. Instructions: Ask students to input prompts that include characters from different cultural backgrounds, genders, and abilities.
3. Output: The AI generates a story based on these diverse prompts.

Discussion Questions:

-   How does the inclusion of diverse characters change the story?
-   What new perspectives did you learn about through the AI-generated story?

Example 2: Inclusive Art and Design Grades Pre-K–12

Use AI to create inclusive artwork or design projects.

Activity:

1. AI Tool: Use AI art generators like DALL·E or Stable Diffusion XL.
2. Instructions: Students input prompts that describe a variety of cultural scenes, traditional clothing, and diverse groups of people.
3. Output: AI generates artwork based on these inclusive prompts.

Discussion Questions:

- How does the AI-generated artwork represent different cultures?
- What elements of the artwork challenge common stereotypes?

Example 3: Analyzing AI-Generated News Articles Grades 3–12

Teach students to critically assess AI-generated news articles for stereotypical representations.

Activity:

1. AI Tool: Use AI news generators like NewsGPT or AIWriter.
2. Instructions: Provide students with AI-generated news articles.
3. Task: Ask students to identify any stereotypical language or representations in the articles.

Discussion Questions:

- What stereotypes did you find in the AI-generated articles?
- How can we ensure that news articles do not reinforce stereotypes?

Example 4: Evaluating AI-Generated Advertisements

Assess AI-generated advertisements for stereotypical depictions.

Activity:

1. AI Tool: Use an AI tool like AdCreative.ai to generate advertisements.
2. Instructions: Students input prompts to create advertisements for products.
3. Task: Evaluate the advertisements for any stereotypical portrayals of gender, race, or age.

Discussion Questions:

- Which stereotypes were most common in the AI-generated ads?
- How would you modify the advertisements to avoid these stereotypes?

Example 5: Role-Playing with AI Chatbots Grades 2–12

Use AI chatbots to role-play scenarios that challenge stereotypes.

Activity:

1. AI Tool: Use AI chatbots on any LLM.
2. Instructions: Students interact with the chatbot, creating scenarios that address and challenge stereotypes (e.g., a chatbot character who defies traditional gender roles).

Discussion Questions:

- How did the chatbot respond to scenarios that challenged stereotypes?
- What did you learn about stereotypes through this interaction?

Example 6: Creating Public Service Announcements (PSAs) Grades 2–12

Use AI to create PSAs that promote diversity and inclusion.

Activity:

1. AI Tool: Use AI video generators like HeyGen or Lumen5.
2. Instructions: Students create scripts for PSAs that highlight the importance of diversity and inclusion.
3. Output: AI helps generate videos based on these scripts.

Discussion Questions:

- How effective are the AI-generated PSAs in challenging stereotypes?
- What message about diversity and inclusion did your PSA convey?

Younger Learners and AI

Introducing younger learners to ethics and recognizing bias can be both engaging and educational. Here are some ideas tailored to elementary school students from GPT-4-128k:

Example 1: Ethical Stories, Grades Kindergarten–2, Ages 5–7

Use stories to illustrate ethical dilemmas and decision-making.

Activity:

1. Read Aloud: Choose age-appropriate books that include ethical dilemmas. Examples include *The Berenstain Bears and the Truth* by Stan and Jan Berenstain or *What If Everybody Did That?* by Ellen Javernick.
2. Discussion: After reading, discuss the story with the students. Ask questions like:
- What was the problem in the story?
- What choices did the characters have?
- What was the best choice and why?

Follow-Up: Have students draw or write about a time they made an ethical decision.

Example 2: Fairy Tales with a Twist, Grades 3–5, Ages 8–10

Goal: Help students recognize bias through familiar stories.

Activity:

1. Classic Fairy Tales: Read a classic fairy tale (e.g., "Cinderella").
2. Discussion: Talk about the characters and their roles. Ask:
- Who are the good and bad characters?
- Why do we think they are good or bad?
1. Twist: Introduce a version of the story from a different perspective (e.g., "The True Story of the Three Little Pigs" by Jon Scieszka).

Follow-Up: Let students create their own version of a fairy tale from another character's perspective.

Example 3: Role-Playing, Grade 1–3, Ages 6–8

Goal: Use role-playing to help students understand ethical choices and bias.

Activity:

1. Scenario Setup: Create simple scenarios where students need to make ethical decisions (e.g., finding a lost toy, sharing resources).
2. Roles: Assign roles to students and let them act out the scenarios.
3. Discussion: After each role-play, discuss the choices made and their consequences.

Follow-Up: Have students write about what they learned from the role-play.

Example 4: Bias Detection Game, Grades 4–6, Ages 9–11

Goal: Teach students to recognize and question bias.

Activity:

1. Pictures and Stories: Show students pictures or read short stories that contain subtle biases (e.g., all doctors in a picture are men, all nurses are women).
2. Discussion: Ask students to identify any patterns or biases they notice.
3. Correction: Discuss how these biases can be corrected (e.g., showing diverse representations).

Follow-Up: Have students draw or write their own unbiased stories or pictures.

Example 5: Ethical AI in Simple Terms, Grades 5–7, Ages 10–12

Goal: Introduce the concept of ethical AI in an accessible way.

Activity:

1. Simple Explanation: Explain that AI helps computers make decisions, but we need to make sure these decisions are fair and kind.
2. Interactive Tools: Use kid-friendly AI tools or apps that demonstrate decision-making (e.g., a simple chatbot that makes ethical choices).

Follow-Up: Let students interact with the tool and discuss their experiences.

Creative Projects

Example 6: Ethics Collage, Grades 2–4, Ages 7–9

Goal: Help students visually explore ethical concepts.

Activity:

1. Materials: Provide magazines, scissors, glue, and poster board.
2. Task: Ask students to create a collage that represents ethical behavior (e.g., sharing, honesty).

Presentation: Have each student present their collage and explain their choices.

Example 6: Bias-Free Storybooks Grade: 3rd to 5th, age: 8-10 years old

Goal: Encourage students to create inclusive and unbiased stories.

Activity:

1. Story Creation: Provide templates for students to write and illustrate their own storybooks.
2. Guidelines: Encourage them to include diverse characters and avoid stereotypes.

Sharing: Allow students to share their books with the class or display them in the school library.

By using these engaging and age-appropriate activities, we can help young learners learn about ethics and recognize bias in a way that is both fun and educational. These foundational lessons will prepare them for more complex ethical decision-making and critical thinking as they grow older.

Chapter Summary

This chapter emphasized the importance of developing ethical learners in the context of AI. As AI becomes increasingly embedded in our lives, it is crucial to teach students to use AI responsibly. The focus is on recognizing biases, understanding ethical frameworks, and challenging stereotypes in AI applications to cultivate digitally aware citizens who ensure technology serves humanity.

Key components of AI ethics, such as moral responsibility, transparency, accountability, privacy, and security, are highlighted. The chapter provided practical examples for educators to instill these values through meaningful learning experiences, case studies, and AI-generated lesson plans. It also addressed the ethical challenges posed by deepfakes and the importance of understanding and mitigating biases in AI systems through activities like bias detection exercises and role-playing scenarios.

Additionally, the chapter offered strategies for teaching younger learners about ethics and bias using age-appropriate activities and creative projects. By incorporating these lessons into the curriculum, educators can help students navigate AI complexities and foster a more ethical and inclusive digital world. The chapter concluded with a call to action for educators to guide AI development in ways that enhance educational outcomes and align with core educational values.

Discussion Questions

1. What strategies can educators use to teach students about recognizing and mitigating biases in AI? Can you share examples of activities or exercises that have been effective in your classroom?
2. How can we effectively incorporate ethical frameworks into AI education for students? What ethical principles do you think are most important for students to understand when working with AI?
3. What are the potential impacts of deepfakes on education and how can we prepare students to handle them responsibly? How can we create lessons that make students aware of the dangers of deepfakes and the importance of verifying information?
4. In what ways can we engage younger learners in discussions about AI ethics and biases? What age-appropriate activities or stories have you found useful in introducing these complex topics to younger students?
5. How can educators ensure that AI tools are used to enhance inclusivity and challenge stereotypes in the classroom? Can you provide examples of AI tools or projects that have successfully promoted diversity and inclusivity in your teaching experience?

Artefact Opportunity

Bias Detection Activity:

Use an AI tool to generate content relevant that is relevant to your subject area/ grade level (e.g., picture of a fairy tale or politician). Analyze the image for potential biases and discuss how these biases could impact different groups within the institution. Propose ways to mitigate these biases.

CHAPTER 9
AI-INFUSED STUDENT PROJECTS

School systems should base their curriculum not on the idea of separate subjects, but on the much more fertile idea of disciplines . . . which makes possible a fluid and dynamic curriculum that is interdisciplinary.
—Sir Ken Robinson, British author,
speaker and international advisor on education

How Can AI-Infused Projects Enhance Learning?

One of my favorite lessons from the past year was an artificial intelligence–infused design thinking lesson I conducted with a group of third-grade students. These students were already engaged in a fascinating unit of inquiry on human body systems, exploring their connections and how to maintain their health. The teachers had done a phenomenal job incorporating hands-on STEM experiences, so I wanted to find a way to use design thinking to further enhance student agency and help them apply their knowledge in a meaningful way.

We started with the core principles of design thinking, focusing on the problem and the user. Given the time constraints and safeguarding and privacy issues around discussing real-life health conditions, we turned to artificial intelligence. Using AI, we generated a fictional character named Michael, complete with a profile and potential challenges stemming from a health condition.

The AI told us that Michael had undergone heart surgery as a baby and, while healthy, needed to be careful at school to maintain his well-being. The students empathized deeply with Michael, and the AI allowed us to "speak" with him, asking questions about his daily life and struggles. This led to brainstorming and iterating on solutions, with the AI providing feedback that challenged students to think critically and refine their ideas. The entire experience was dynamic and student-centered, highlighting the interconnectedness of body systems and the importance of empathy in problem-solving. It was a powerful demonstration of how AI and design thinking can empower students to become creative and compassionate problem solvers.

John Hendrickse, head of Primary Technology and Innovation (TI)
Victoria Shanghai Academy, Hong Kong

MIKE

Mike was born with a hole in the wall that separates the two main pumping chambers of his heart.

He has undergone a surgery to repair the defect, but he still needs to be cautious about his heart health.

Jacob is a remarkable 8-year-old boy who loves being active and imaginative. He wants to come up with a creative solution that helps him take care of his heart and inspires other children who may have similar heart conditions

MORE ABOUT MIKE

Mike is an energetic and imaginative child who enjoys outdoor adventures, playing soccer with friends, and creating imaginative stories.

QUESTIONS TO ASK

How can we help Mike take care of his heart while staying active?

What reminders or systems can we create to support Mike in taking breaks and following his medication routine?

How can we monitor Mike's heart health and provide personalized recommendations?

What can we do to raise awareness among Mike's classmates and create an inclusive environment for children with similar heart conditions?

Project-Based Learning (PBL)

The Buck Institute for Education defines *project-based learning* (PBL) as "a teaching method in which students learn by actively engaging in real-world and personally meaningful projects." PBL immerses students in authentic problems and challenges, fostering a deeper connection to the material and enhancing their motivation to learn. Unlike traditional rote learning, PBL emphasizes active, hands-on experiences that require critical thinking, collaboration, and creativity. Research has shown that PBL can significantly improve student outcomes, including higher retention rates, better problem-solving skills, and increased engagement. Research from Almulla (2020) found that the project-based learning (PBL) approach significantly enhances student engagement by fostering collaborative, disciplinary, iterative, and authentic learning. Using a questionnaire and structural equation modeling (SEM) to analyze data from 124 teachers, the results demonstrated that PBL effectively supports collaborative knowledge sharing and discussion, making it a highly recommended method for educational use in universities.

In this chapter, we explore a series of innovative projects that harness the power of AI to augment student learning and creativity across various domains. These project ideas are designed to inspire educators and students, offering a springboard into the world of AI tailored for grades pre-K to 12.

As you explore these projects, please note that direct links to specific digital AI tools are not provided, as we do not endorse any specific AI tool. The materials and projects presented here are designed to be agnostic to any particular AI digital tool, allowing educators the flexibility to choose the resources that best fit their classroom needs. We encourage educators to use these projects as a guide to explore the vast array of AI resources available. With a simple search, you can find numerous AI tools that will fit the needs of your classroom and comply with your school's technology policies.

From using AI to compose unique pieces of music to employing AI tools to generate captivating graphics, these projects are designed to immerse students in the practical aspects of AI technology. By engaging directly with these applications, students will not only develop a foundational understanding of AI but also experience first-hand how it can be applied to real-world creative tasks.

Each project is structured to be both educational and exciting, providing students with a dynamic learning environment where they can experiment with AI capabilities. This hands-on approach aims to spark curiosity and inspire a deeper interest in the fields of technology and innovation, preparing students for a future where AI plays a central role.

Reminder about Data Protection

Before we begin, please be aware of data protection, where everyone from students to faculty needs to feel confident that their personal information is safe and handled with care. Only collect and use the minimum amount of student data necessary for the AI tool to function effectively. Be transparent with students and parents about how AI is used in the classroom and what data is collected. Obtain informed consent when necessary.

Image generated by DALL·E 3, 2024

Educators should be aware that children under 13 are entitled to specific data protection measures, particularly when using AI tools. To ensure compliance, it is advisable that children are not required to input any personal data when using such tools. The General Data Protection Regulation (GDPR) emphasizes the need for clear and plain language when communicating with children to ensure their understanding of how their data will be used. Additionally, the UK's Data Protection Act 2018 sets the age limit for children's consent to data processing in the context of online services at 13 years.

Therefore, educators should take steps to ensure that AI tools used by children under 13 do not collect their personal data, and if data input is necessary, parental consent should be obtained. They should also be transparent with students and parents about how AI is used in the classroom and what data is collected. Obtain informed consent when necessary.

For children who are *under 13,* teachers can protect student privacy by using school accounts on classroom devices for AI tool access. This avoids the need for students to enter personal information and complies with age restrictions. By centralizing access to AI tools, educators enhance digital learning security.

Educators are encouraged to set up interactive learning stations with devices logged into their school accounts, providing a secure way for students to explore AI without personal data concerns. This approach promotes a safe and engaging learning environment aligned with data protection standards.

Image generated by DALL·E 3, 2024

Remember, the aim is to cultivate a sense of wonder and a foundational understanding of ethical AI use in our students, equipping them with the skills to navigate and shape the dynamically changing future. Let's prepare our young learners to become not just consumers of technology but also innovators and critical thinkers in an AI-infused world.

Here are some project ideas we can develop to integrate AI usage with our learners:

AI-Assisted Music and Sound Design Projects

AI can play a significant role in music education and sound design projects, making these fields more accessible to students and providing them with tools to explore and create in new ways:

Music Composition Tools: AI-powered tools can assist students in composing music by suggesting chord progressions, melodies, and harmonizations based on the genre or mood they want to explore. These tools can serve as a virtual collaborator, offering ideas that students can accept, modify, or reject.

Image generated by DALL·E 3, 2024

Sound Editing and Production: AI can simplify the process of sound editing and production, making it easier for students to experiment with creating their own audio projects. For instance, AI tools can automatically adjust levels, mix tracks, or even suggest adjustments to improve the sound quality of recordings.

Exploration of Music History and Styles: AI can generate examples of music from different periods or cultures, helping students explore a wide range of musical styles and contexts. This can be particularly inspiring for students, leading them to incorporate diverse influences into their own creations.

These AI-enhanced tools not only support the technical aspects of music and sound design but also help to stimulate creativity, providing students with a broad palette of sounds and styles to inspire their own artistic expressions. This approach fosters a deeper understanding and appreciation of music and sound engineering, while also equipping students with practical skills in these fields.

AI-Powered Exploration of Healthy Habits and Nutrition

AI can be a powerful ally in teaching students about healthy habits and nutrition, making these crucial topics more engaging and personalized:

Exploring the Science of Food and Digestion: AI can help students inquire more deeply into the science behind food and digestion. Interactive simulations can illustrate how the body processes different nutrients, the role of gut health, and the impact of food choices on overall well-being.

Interactive Food Journals: AI can enhance traditional food journals by providing real-time feedback and insights into eating patterns. Students can track their food intake, and AI algorithms can analyze the data to identify areas for improvement and suggest healthier alternatives.

Exploring Global Cuisines and Dietary Traditions: AI can introduce students to a diverse range of cuisines and dietary traditions from around the world. By analyzing cultural food practices, students can gain a broader understanding of nutrition and develop an appreciation for different culinary approaches to healthy living.

These AI-enhanced tools can empower students to take ownership of their health and well-being, making learning about nutrition and healthy habits a more interactive and personalized experience.

AI-Powered Exploration of Academic Honesty and Ethics

AI can be infused into projects to engage high school students in discussions about academic honesty and ethics, making these crucial topics more relevant and thought-provoking:

Interactive Case Studies: AI can power interactive case studies that present students with realistic scenarios involving plagiarism, cheating, and other ethical dilemmas. Students can analyze these situations, make decisions, and explore the consequences of their choices in a safe and engaging environment.

Virtual Debates and Discussions: AI can facilitate virtual debates and discussions on ethical issues related to academic integrity. AI-powered chatbots can present different perspectives, challenge students' assumptions, and encourage critical thinking about the complexities of ethical decision-making.

Exploring the History and Philosophy of Ethics: AI can help students explore the history and philosophy of ethics, providing access to a wealth of information and diverse perspectives. Students can research different ethical theories, analyze real-world examples of ethical dilemmas, and develop their own frameworks for ethical decision-making.

Analyzing the Impact of Technology on Academic Integrity: AI can be used to analyze how technology has impacted academic integrity, both positively and negatively. Students can explore the use of plagiarism-detection software, the rise of contract cheating websites, and the ethical implications of using AI tools for academic work.

Connecting Ethics to Real-World Careers and Social Issues: AI can facilitate discussions about how ethical principles apply to real-world careers and social issues. Students can research ethical codes of conduct in various professions, analyze ethical dilemmas faced by professionals, and explore the role of ethics in addressing social challenges.

These AI-infused projects can empower students to develop a strong sense of ethical responsibility, fostering a deeper understanding of academic honesty and its importance in both academic and professional contexts.

To help you get started, please use the following QR code to access a collection of ready-to-use project examples that you can easily print and implement in your classroom.

Chapter Summary

This chapter explored the integration of AI into project-based learning (PBL) to create engaging and meaningful educational experiences. PBL, as defined by the Buck Institute for Education, involves students actively engaging in real-world projects that enhance their critical thinking, collaboration, and creativity. Research, such as Almulla's 2020 study, shows that PBL significantly improves student engagement and learning outcomes.

The chapter discussed a variety of innovative AI projects for students from Pre-K to 12, designed to inspire and provide practical skills. These projects encourage students to use AI for tasks like music composition, sound editing, and graphic design, helping them understand and apply AI in creative ways. The projects are tool-agnostic, allowing educators flexibility in choosing resources that fit their classroom needs. More AI infused projects can be found in the appendices.

A key focus is on data protection and ethical AI use. Educators are advised to use school accounts for AI tools, ensuring compliance with data privacy regulations, especially for students under 13. The chapter also emphasizes the importance of teaching students to fact-check AI-generated material, fostering critical thinking and discernment. Fact-checking guidelines and resources such as FactCheck.org, Google Scholar, and PolitiFact are provided to support this endeavor. Ultimately, the chapter aimed to prepare students to be responsible and innovative thinkers in an AI-driven world.

Discussion Questions

1. How can AI be effectively integrated into Project-Based Learning (PBL) to enhance student engagement and learning outcomes? What are some specific examples of successful AI-infused PBL projects you can envision or have implemented?

2. What strategies can educators use to ensure data privacy and ethical use of AI tools in the classroom, especially for students under 13? How do you address concerns about data protection and informed consent in your own teaching practice?

3. In what ways can AI tools be used to foster creativity and critical thinking in subjects beyond traditional STEM fields? Can you share ideas for AI projects in subjects like history, literature, or the arts?

4. What are the challenges and solutions in teaching students to fact-check AI-generated material? How can we incorporate fact-checking skills into everyday classroom activities to develop students' critical thinking abilities?

5. How can educators balance the use of AI tools with other teaching resources to create a well-rounded educational experience? What are some best practices for blending AI technology with hands-on, interactive learning experiences?

Artefact Opportunity

Design an AI-Infused Project:

Create a project-based learning activity that incorporates AI tools, focusing on a topic relevant to your curriculum. Plan the project, implement it with students, and evaluate its impact on learning outcomes.

CHAPTER 10

ENHANCING HUMANITY:
UTILIZING AI TO FOSTER EMPATHY, CREATIVITY, AND CRITICAL THINKING

Responsible AI is not just about liability–it's about ensuring
what you are building is enabling human flourishing.
–Rumman Chowdhury, CEO at Parity AI

How Can We Elevate Essential Human Skills in an AI-Driven World?

In an AI-driven world, the challenge is not solely to integrate AI into our daily lives and professions ethically, but to utilize its potential to enhance our humanity. As AI technologies continue to evolve, the focus should shift toward how these tools can amplify essential human skills such as creativity, critical thinking, and empathy, rather than replace them.

We know AI's capability to process vast amounts of data and identify patterns can free humans from repetitive tasks, but how can we use AI for more creative and critical pursuits? For instance, AI can assist in brainstorming sessions by generating diverse ideas and solutions, which can then be critically evaluated and refined by human minds. This symbiosis of AI and human intellect fosters a new realm of creativity and innovation. AI can also enhance critical thinking by providing access to a wealth of information and perspectives, enabling individuals to analyze and synthesize data more effectively.

Integrating insights from fields such as neuroscience, psychology, and education with AI development can create tools that not only solve technical problems but also enrich human lives and societies. In this chapter, we explore the myriad ways AI can be leveraged to cultivate these essential human skills, setting the stage for a future where technology and humanity advance hand in hand.

As we navigate this AI world, remember that we are all lifelong learners. This chapter isn't about machines replacing us; it's about how they can help us cultivate the skills that define us at our best. Together, let's discover how AI can be leveraged not only to augment our abilities but also to enrich our human experience. We will explore how AI can help us push the boundaries of what it means to be creative, thoughtful, collaborative, and compassionate human beings.

The Importance of Empathy

Empathy is crucial in fostering intercultural understanding, as it allows individuals to genuinely appreciate and respect diverse perspectives and experiences. By cultivating empathy, we can bridge cultural divides and build more inclusive and harmonious communities.

Empathy, often seen as the cornerstone of human connection and understanding, is a critical skill that AI can help nurture. By

Image generated by DALL·E 3, 2024

leveraging AI technologies, we can develop experiences for learners that promote empathy, enabling individuals to better understand and relate to others. This is particularly important in our increasingly globalized world, where diverse cultures and perspectives intersect daily.

Here are some examples of projects that develop empathy in our learners generated by GPT-4-128k (https://poe.com/s/mzuchG9OOjyvkSggOxr7):

---

1. Community Service Project

Suggested grade levels: middle school to high school (grades 6–12)

Ages: 11–18 years

Goal: Students will engage with local community services to understand and address the needs of diverse groups.

Project Description:

- **Research Phase:** Students research local community organizations and identify a group they are interested in supporting (e.g., elderly, homeless, disabled).
- **Interaction Phase:** Students volunteer their time or organize a drive (e.g., food, clothes, books) to support the chosen community group.
- **Reflection Phase:** Students write reflective essays or present their experiences and the emotional insights they gained about the lives of the people they helped.

Skills Developed: Empathy, social awareness, communication, teamwork.

2. Cultural Exchange Program

Suggested Grade Levels: Middle School to High School (Grades 6-12)

Ages: 11-18 years

Goal: To develop empathy and understanding for different cultural backgrounds among students.

Project Description:

- **Preparation Phase:** Students are paired with a student from a different cultural background and tasked with learning about each other's customs, traditions, and daily lives.
- **Exchange Phase:** Each student spends a day or a class period "in the shoes" of their partner, attempting to live according to their partner's cultural practices.
- **Presentation Phase:** Students create presentations about their experiences and what they learned about the challenges and beauties of another culture.

Skills Developed: Cross-cultural empathy, communication, adaptability.

3. Empathy Through Literature

Suggested grade levels: upper elementary to high school (grades 4–12)

Ages: 9–18 years

Goal: Use literature as a mirror and window to explore different emotional experiences and perspectives.

Project Description:

- **Reading Phase:** Students read a novel or a series of short stories featuring protagonists from diverse backgrounds.
- **Discussion Phase:** Through guided discussions, students explore the characters' emotions, motivations, and decisions.
- **Creative Phase:** Students write a short story or a diary entry from the perspective of one of the characters, focusing on capturing their emotional journey.

Skills Developed: Perspective-taking, critical thinking, creative expression.

4. Peer Mentoring Program

Suggested grade levels: middle school to high school (grades 6–12)

Ages: 11–18 years

Goal: Foster empathy and support among students by setting up a peer mentoring system.

Project Description:

- **Training Phase:** Students receive training on active listening, basic counseling, and support techniques.
- **Mentoring Phase:** Older students are paired with younger ones, helping them with academic or social issues.
- **Evaluation Phase:** Mentors and mentees provide feedback on the program, discussing improvements and successes in understanding and supporting each other.

Skills Developed: Empathy, leadership, communication, responsibility.

Developing Empathy Through the U.N.'s 17 Sustainable Development Goals (SDGs) in AI Project-Based Learning (PBL)

Leveraging AI to develop PBL that embraces an interdisciplinary approach offers a more authentic learning experience. By integrating diverse subject areas, PBL encourages students to tackle complex, real-world challenges, such as those outlined in the United Nations' 17 Sustainable Development Goals (SDGs), from multiple perspectives, leading to more comprehensive and impactful solutions. Crucially, these projects can foster empathy as an understanding that addressing the needs and feelings of others is fundamental to driving effective and compassionate action toward achieving these goals.

The United Nations' 17 Sustainable Development Goals (SDGs) are a universal call to action to end poverty, protect the planet, and ensure that all people enjoy peace and prosperity by 2030. Addressing the U.N.'s 17 SDGs requires a holistic and empathetic approach.

Here's are some examples of project outlines that address some of the UNs SDG's generated by GPT-4-128k:

No Poverty and Zero Hunger (Goals 1 & 2)

Project: Community Engagement for Hunger Relief

Students research the root causes of poverty and hunger in their community by engaging directly with affected individuals and families. They then organize initiatives such as food drives or community kitchens, using their first-hand experiences to inform and enhance these efforts. The project not only addresses immediate needs but also promotes a deeper understanding among students of the socioeconomic factors contributing to these issues.

Quality Education (Goal 4)

Project: Literacy and Learning Support

This project involves students in setting up or participating in programs that support educational access in underserved parts of their community. They might create tutoring programs, donate books, or set up educational workshops. By interacting with and teaching peers or younger students, participants develop empathy by understanding the diverse educational challenges and barriers others face.

Gender Equality (Goal 5)

Project: Voices for Equality

Students conduct interviews and gather stories from people of different genders facing discrimination. They use this information to create powerful narratives through documentaries, presentations, or social media campaigns aimed at advocating for gender equality. This project helps students empathize with those affected by gender-based injustices and raises awareness in the broader community.

Clean Water and Sanitation (Goal 6)

Project: Water Life Cycle Study

Students analyze the impact of water scarcity on communities, possibly partnering with a community in a different part of the world through digital tools. They can develop water-saving solutions or awareness campaigns based on their studies and interactions. Understanding the daily struggles related to water scarcity promotes empathy and inspires innovative solutions.

Reduced Inequalities (Goal 10)

Project: Bridging Diverse Worlds

This involves creating events or platforms where stories from marginalized or underrepresented groups are highlighted. Students could organize art exhibits, storytelling sessions, or discussion forums that foster a deeper understanding of the inequalities these groups face. Engaging directly with diverse communities enhances students' empathy and drives a commitment to advocating for equity.

Climate Action (Goal 13)

Project: Environmental Empathy Exhibits

Students engage with local environmental scientists and activists to understand the impacts of climate change on their community. They then translate these insights into educational exhibits or interactive workshops for the public, aiming to personalize the effects of climate change and foster a community-wide empathetic response.

Peace, Justice, and Strong Institutions (Goal 16)

Project: Paths to Peace

Students explore historical and contemporary issues related to peace and justice through research and interviews with peacekeepers, justice workers, and community leaders. They organize public forums or school assemblies to share their findings and advocate for peaceful solutions to conflicts, fostering an environment of understanding and empathy within their community.

By integrating empathy into projects aimed at the SDGs, educators can help students not only understand these global challenges but also feel empowered to contribute to sustainable solutions. These empathetic approaches ensure that students are not just passive learners but active participants in shaping a more just and sustainable world.

AI Tools to Enhance Creativity

AI can significantly enhance the human quality of creativity by acting as a collaborative partner that expands our imaginative horizons and provides fresh perspectives. AI tools can generate novel ideas, suggest unique combinations, and offer new ways of thinking that might not occur to humans alone. For instance, AI-powered platforms like OpenAI's GPT-4 can assist writers by generating story prompts or crafting dialogue.

When writing this book on AI-powered pedagogy, I found invaluable thought partners in bots I subscribe to on Poe.com, including GPT-4, Gemini 1.5 Pro, Claude-3-Opus, GPT-4-128k, and GPT-4o, to name a few. These interactions, guided by the design thinking process, helped me refine ideas, gain diverse perspectives, and enhance the content by engaging in dynamic exchanges and iterative dialogues with AI models, ultimately enriching the creativity and quality of the final output.

Generative image AI tools like DALL·E represent a significant advancement in enhancing human creativity within the visual arts. These tools are capable of producing highly detailed and imaginative images based on textual descriptions, enabling artists to bring their concepts to life with unprecedented ease and precision. For instance, generative AI can produce unique and visually stunning

Image generated by DALL·E 3, 2024

representations of ideas, allowing artists to experiment with and visualize concepts that might be difficult or time-consuming to create manually. By providing rapid visual prototypes, these AI tools inspire new artistic directions and help artists push the boundaries of their creativity. They enable exploration of innovative compositions that blend elements in novel ways, thus expanding the possibilities within the realm of visual arts.

In music, AI can compose original pieces, suggest chord progressions, and create symphonies, enabling musicians to explore new genres and harmonies. Tools like AIVA (Artificial Intelligence Virtual Artist) allow composers to input basic parameters and receive fully orchestrated compositions that can be further refined and personalized. This not only accelerates the creative process but also opens up new avenues for musical innovation and collaboration.

AI tools can be incredibly effective for creative problem-solving because they can process vast amounts of data quickly, identify patterns, and generate innovative solutions that might not be immediately apparent to humans. These tools can process large amounts of data quickly, visualize connections between ideas, and provide intelligent insights that might not be immediately apparent. This allows individuals and teams to focus more on refining and developing their ideas, ultimately enhancing their critical thinking and creativity.

Mural AI is an advanced collaborative tool designed to enhance brainstorming sessions through a virtual whiteboard and real-time collaboration. Mural AI offers features such as idea clustering, smart templates, and automated insights. During a brainstorming session, for example, Mural AI can automatically group related ideas and highlight key themes, helping teams to organize their thoughts more effectively and identify potential connections between concepts. This structured yet flexible environment enables learners to focus on exploring creative solutions and refining their ideas. Importantly, Mural AI supports design thinking methodologies by facilitating empathy mapping, ideation, prototyping, and testing, making it an essential tool for creative problem-solving.

Here are the key capabilities of Mural AI:

1. **Generate Mind Maps:** Users can create mind maps instantly by providing a central idea or prompt. Mural AI will generate a full mind map with related concepts and ideas branching out.

2. **Generate Content:** Leveraging natural language prompts, Mural AI can generate ideas, visuals, questions, hypotheses, and other content directly on the Mural canvas to fuel brainstorming and problem-solving sessions.

3. **Summarize:** It can quickly summarize text, sticky notes, and other content on a Mural board to synthesize key points and ideas.

4. **Cluster Ideas:** Mural AI can automatically cluster and group related sticky notes based on themes or topics, accelerating the affinity mapping process.

5. **Integrate with Microsoft Copilot:** Mural integrates with Microsoft 365 Copilot, allowing users to leverage Copilot's natural language capabilities to find murals, summarize content, generate ideas and streamline collaboration workflows.

Similarly, Miro Assist (formerly Miro AI) provides a robust platform for creative problem-solving with its interactive online whiteboard. Miro Assist is an AI-powered assistant integrated into the Miro visual collaboration platform. Its main purpose is to augment and accelerate the creative and problem-solving workflows of teams using Miro's digital whiteboards and templates.

Here are some key things Miro Assist can do:

1. **Generate Content and Ideas:** Miro Assist can generate ideas, content, and visuals based on text prompts or the context of the Miro board. This includes creating mind maps, diagrams, presentations, images, and more from scratch or expanding on existing elements

2. **Provide Intelligent Suggestions:** It can analyze the content on a Miro board and provide relevant suggestions, insights, and next steps to further ideation, planning, and execution.
3. **Automate Tasks:** Miro Assist can automate repetitive tasks like summarizing notes, drafting action items, or cleaning up visuals, saving teams time and effort.
4. **Enhance Collaboration:** By generating content and facilitating ideation, Miro Assist aims to enhance real-time collaboration and alignment within distributed teams working on Miro boards

Both Mural AI and Miro Assist are deeply rooted in design thinking principles, supporting stages such as empathizing with users, defining problems, ideating, prototyping, and testing solutions. However, a key difference lies in their focus. Mural is specifically tailored for visual collaboration and brainstorming, offering a wide array of templates and tools to help users create and organize ideas effectively. Miro, on the other hand, is a more versatile collaboration platform, suitable for a wider range of purposes, including planning, prototyping, and design

By leveraging the capabilities of tools such as Mural AI and Miro AI, students and professionals alike can transform their brainstorming sessions into dynamic, productive experiences that foster creativity and critical thinking. These tools provide the structure and support needed to explore new ideas and solve complex problems effectively while adhering to design thinking methodologies that ensure solutions are user centered and innovative.

By handling repetitive tasks and providing creative suggestions, AI allows humans to focus more on refining and innovating their work. This symbiotic relationship between AI and human creativity not only enhances our artistic capabilities but also fosters a deeper understanding and appreciation of the creative process itself.

Using AI to Sharpen Critical Thinking

In our current world, where we are constantly bombarded with information, critical thinking has become an indispensable skill. AI can be instrumental in developing this skill by providing tools for data analysis and visualization. Learners can interact with AI-powered simulations that present complex scenarios and encourage them to analyze data, identify patterns, and draw informed conclusions. AI can also help combat misinformation by identifying bias and fake news, empowering individuals to critically evaluate information before forming opinions. Additionally, AI-driven debate platforms can provide a safe space for learners to engage in constructive discourse, refining their arguments and understanding different perspectives.

Lesson Ideas for Sharpening Critical Thinking Using AI (from GPT-4-128k)

Lesson Outline: Fact or Fiction – Verifying AI Outputs for Bias and Accuracy
Grade Level: 9–12
Subject: Media Literacy/Information Technology
Materials Needed:

- AI content generation tools (e.g., ChatGPT)
- Internet and research databases access
- Fact-checking guidelines and resources
- Worksheets for recording findings

Lesson Overview:

In this project-based inquiry, students will critically assess the reliability of AI-generated content. They will interact with AI to produce information, then use research skills to verify the accuracy and uncover any biases.

Lesson Activities:

Introduction to AI in Media

Examples of Fake News and Dubious Claims

1. Political Misinformation:
Example: During an election period, an AI-generated article falsely claims that a candidate has withdrawn from the race due to health issues, potentially affecting voter behavior.

2. Health Misinformation:
Example: An AI system spreads information that a certain herb is a cure for Covid-19, despite no scientific backing. This type of misinformation can lead to dangerous health behaviors and public panic.

3. Financial Fraud:
Example: Fake news generated by AI claims that a certain company is on the verge of bankruptcy, leading to a stock market manipulation scheme where traders sell off their stocks rapidly, causing real financial damage.

Examples of AI Hallucinations

- Historical Inaccuracies:
- Example: An AI, when asked about historical events, might "hallucinate" details, such as incorrectly stating that Napoleon Bonaparte fought in World War I.
- Scientific Data:
- Example: An AI tool designed to assist with homework might generate a plausible-sounding but entirely incorrect explanation of a scientific principle, like stating that water boils at 70 degrees Celsius.
- Biographical Errors:
- Example: An AI generating biographical content might create a profile for a celebrity that includes false relationships or achievements, like claiming a famous actress won an Oscar for a movie she wasn't in.
- Geographical Errors:
- Example: In generating descriptions of locations, an AI might confuse landmarks, claiming, for example, that the Eiffel Tower is located in Rome.

Each of these examples underscores the potential risks associated with uncritically accepting AI-generated content. Whether it's through malicious intent (as with some fake news) or the inherent limitations of AI (as with hallucinations), these inaccuracies can have real-world consequences. Educators and students must be equipped to recognize and investigate the veracity of such information, reinforcing the need for robust digital literacy skills in an AI-driven world.

Teaching Learners How to Fact-Check

Many learners are now using AI tools to augment their learning, but this comes with the challenge of navigating a world overflowing with information. It is crucial for students to develop strong fact-checking skills and learn to critically evaluate the outputs of AI tools.

As we incorporate the use of AI tools in PBL scenarios, the ability to fact-check AI-generated material is rapidly becoming an essential skill. While AI opens up new avenues for creativity and efficiency, it can also produce inaccurate or biased information. Without proper guidance, students may rely on these flawed outputs, leading to misguided conclusions and learning outcomes. By incorporating fact-checking skills into AI-infused projects, educators can ensure that students develop critical thinking abilities and a discerning approach to digital content. This not only enhances the quality of their work but also prepares them to navigate a world where AI-generated information is ubiquitous.

Figure 10.1 outline some fact-checking guidelines for students.

Figure 10.1:

Fact Checking Guidelines

FACT-CHECKING GUIDELINES

ANNOTATE DRAFTS WITH SOURCES

1 Ensure you annotate each fact to prepare for fact-checking.

PROVIDE SOURCES PACKAGE

2 Provide primary sources, interview transcripts, notes, and other research materials in a "research package" for the fact-checker.

USE A VARIETY OF SOURCES

3 Use a variety of sources to corroborate facts (triangulation).

CONSULT CREDIBLE OUTLETS

4 Consult professional news agencies and credible outlets, which have editorial standards and fact-checking resources.

CHECK FOR BIAS

5 Be aware of potential biases in sources and check for confirmation bias.

EVALUATE SOURCE

6 Evaluate sources based on criteria like accuracy, authority, objectivity, currency, and purpose (CRAAP test).

CHECK GUIDELINES FROM CREDIBLE SOURCES

7 Some outlets provide checklists or written guidelines for journalists on preparing materials for fact-checking.

The CRAAP test originated from librarians at California State University and has been a widely adopted too for evaluating the reliability of information source across academic disciplines, using five criteria:

- **Currency** refers to the timeliness and up-to-dateness of the information source. It evaluates how recent the information is and whether it reflects the latest developments or research on the topic. Relevant questions include the publication date, whether the source has been revised or updated, and if the links are functional.
- **Relevance** assesses the importance and applicability of the information source to your specific needs or research question. It considers whether the content directly supports your argument and is written for the appropriate audience level and if you have consulted a variety of sources.
- **Authority** examines the credibility and expertise of the source's creator or publisher. Key factors are the author's qualifications, affiliations, and reputation in the field and whether the source is from a trustworthy organization or has undergone peer-review.
- **Accuracy** evaluates the reliability, truthfulness, and correctness of the content. Signs of accuracy include citations for sources of evidence, corroboration with other sources, a lack of errors, and neutral tone without bias or persuasive intent.
- **Purpose** considers the reason the information source exists and the motivations behind its creation. It examines whether the purpose is to inform, persuade, sell, entertain, or promote a particular ideology or bias, and if the author's intentions are clearly stated.

The CRAAP test helps educators and students determine the trustworthiness of research sources by evaluating their reliability.

Fact-Checking Resources

These websites were found on Perplexity, rewritten by GPT-4-128k, and all verified by me!

- **FactCheck.org:** A project of the Annenberg Public Policy Center that checks the factual accuracy of statements made by major U.S. political players in the form of TV ads, debates, speeches, interviews, and news releases.
- **Google Scholar (scholar.google.com):**
  Useful for finding academic papers and research to verify scientific claims and data.
- **PolitiFact (politifact.com):**
  An independent fact-checking website that rates the accuracy of claims by elected officials and others who speak up in American politics.
- **Reuters Fact Check (reuters.com/fact-check):**
  Provides fact-checking on global news stories and viral claims

---

Here is an example of a lessons that teaches learners how to fact check from GPT-4-128k:

AI Interaction and Data Collection

Students work in small groups, using AI tools to collect information on specific topics. They record the AI's responses for further analysis.

Independent Research and Verification

Students independently verify the AI-generated information using credible sources. They identify and note any discrepancies or biases.

Group Analysis and Presentation

Each group analyzes their findings, focusing on instances where AI content was biased or incorrect. They prepare a presentation to share their insights with the class.

Class Discussion on Findings

Groups present their analysis, fostering a class-wide discussion on the challenges of relying on AI for accurate information and the strategies for effective fact-checking.

> **Reflective Essays**
>
> As a follow-up, students write essays reflecting on their experiences, the importance of critical evaluation of AI-generated content, and the role of AI in modern media.
>
> This inductive inquiry encourages students to engage deeply with the material, fostering skills in critical thinking, research, and collaborative learning as they navigate the complexities of AI-generated information.

Being part of this dynamic field at such a transformative time is exhilarating. I look forward to seeing how continued advancements in AI will further refine our pedagogical strategies and enrich our students' educational journeys. This shift in education isn't just about adopting new tools; it's about fundamentally redefining the essence of how we teach and learn.

By integrating insights from various fields, we can use AI tools that not only enhance our intrinsic human qualities but also contribute to a more just, inclusive, and empathetic world. As we advance in AI technology, it is imperative that we prioritize empathy and human connection, ensuring that AI serves as a force for good in society.

Chapter Summary

This chapter explored how AI can be used to enhance essential human skills such as empathy, creativity, and critical thinking. In an AI-driven world, the goal is not merely to integrate AI ethically into our lives but to utilize its potential to enrich our humanity.

The chapter discussed practical examples of how AI can elevate empathy through project-based learning (PBL) that integrates interdisciplinary approaches. Projects such as community service, cultural exchanges, and empathy through literature are highlighted for their potential to foster empathy among students.

AI's capacity to process large amounts of data and identify patterns frees humans from repetitive tasks, allowing us to concentrate on more creative pursuits. For example, AI can enhance brainstorming sessions by generating diverse ideas and solutions, which humans can then critically evaluate and refine, fostering innovative problem-solving. Additionally, AI tools like Mural AI and Miro Assist enhance creative problem-solving and critical thinking through features such as idea clustering, smart templates, and real-time collaboration.

By integrating AI into educational practices, we can create tools that not only solve technical problems but also enrich human lives and societies. This chapter emphasized the importance of developing empathy, creativity, and critical thinking in learners, preparing them to navigate and shape an AI-driven world responsibly. The ultimate aim is to use AI to augment our abilities and enrich our human experience, fostering a more just, inclusive, and empathetic society.

Discussion Questions

1. How can AI tools be effectively integrated into project-based learning (PBL) to enhance empathy among students? What specific AI tools or ideas do you think are most effective for fostering empathy in students? Can you share any experiences or examples?

2. In what ways can AI support and enhance creative problem-solving in the classroom? How have collaborative tools such as Mural AI and Miro Assist impacted your approach to teaching creativity and critical thinking? Can you provide examples of successful projects?

3. How can educators develop students' critical thinking skills when using AI tools? What strategies do you employ to ensure students are critically evaluating AI-generated content and not just passively accepting it?

4. How can interdisciplinary approaches in PBL, supported by AI, address broader societal goals such as the United Nations' Sustainable Development Goals (SDGs)? Can you share any examples of interdisciplinary projects that have successfully integrated AI to tackle real-world problems and promote social justice and sustainability?

Artefact Opportunity

Empathy-Building Project:

Develop a project that uses AI to foster empathy among students, such as creating a digital story from the perspective of a marginalized group. Present the project and discuss how AI can enhance empathy and understanding within the school community.

Final words

As we conclude *AI-Powered Pedagogy: Redefining Education*, it's time to reflect on the journey we've undertaken together. This book has aimed to empower educators with the knowledge, tools, and confidence to integrate artificial intelligence into teaching practices effectively. By exploring the transformative potential of AI, we have highlighted how it can enhance educational methodologies, support educators, and enrich student learning experiences.

Key Takeaways

1. Institutional Frameworks:

- **Enabling Innovation:** We examined how institutional frameworks can support innovation and integrity, emphasizing the need for evolving, unified AI policies to ensure fair, ethical, and inclusive AI use in education.
- **Ethical Considerations:** The importance of maintaining ethical standards and academic integrity in AI integration was underscored, with practical strategies and frameworks provided to guide educators.

2. Educator Engagement:

- **Stages of AI Adoption:** We mapped the journey of AI adoption, outlining the stages from Survive to Arrive, and provided practical tips and case studies to help educators navigate this process.
- **Streamlining Workflow:** AI's potential to enhance educator workflow and creativity was explored, showcasing tools and techniques to automate administrative tasks and foster innovative teaching practices.
- **Crafting Effective Prompts:** The IDEAS framework was introduced to help educators move beyond static prompt libraries, emphasizing the art of crafting and iteratively refining prompts for meaningful interactions with AI tools.

3. Learner-Centric AI Use:

- **Developing Ethical Learners:** The ethical use of AI was discussed, focusing on teaching students to recognize and mitigate biases, challenge stereotypes, and navigate the digital world responsibly.
- **AI-Infused Projects:** We explored project-based learning (PBL) enhanced by AI, offering practical project ideas to engage students and develop critical thinking, creativity, and empathy.
- **Enhancing Humanity:** The book emphasized the importance of leveraging AI to cultivate essential human skills, such as empathy, creativity, and critical thinking, and highlighted interdisciplinary approaches to address broader societal goals.

As you take what you have learned here back to your school system or classroom, the following are some next steps to help you continue to grow your knowledge and confidence in using AI to enrich your curriculum.

Next Steps

1. Continuous Professional Development:

- Engage in ongoing professional development to stay updated on AI advancements and best practices. Participate in workshops, webinars, and collaborative learning communities focused on AI in education.

2. Ethical Considerations:

- Implement and regularly review ethical guidelines and policies for AI use in your institution. Foster a culture of transparency, accountability, and inclusivity in AI practices.

3. Curriculum Integration:

- Integrate AI tools into your curriculum thoughtfully, ensuring they enhance pedagogical goals and support student learning. Use the projects and examples provided in this book as a starting point to develop your own AI-infused lessons.

4. Student Empowerment:

- Encourage students to use AI responsibly and creatively. Teach them critical thinking and fact-checking skills to navigate AI-generated content and promote ethical digital citizenship.

5. Collaborative Efforts:

- Collaborate with colleagues, administrators, and the broader educational community to share insights, resources, and best practices for AI integration. Foster a supportive network to enhance AI-powered pedagogy collectively.

By embracing these next steps, educators can harness the full potential of AI to create dynamic, engaging, and inclusive learning environments. The journey of AI-powered pedagogy is ongoing, and together, we can redefine education to better prepare our students for the future. Thank you for embarking on this transformative journey with me. Let's continue to innovate, inspire, and empower through the power of AI.

A Personal Note

Throughout my career as an educator and educational consultant, I have had the privilege of witnessing the incredible impact that innovative teaching practices can have on students' lives. Writing this book has been a deeply personal journey for me, driven by my passion for leveraging technology to enhance learning and my commitment to supporting educators in their professional growth.

I remember the first time I introduced AI tools into my workshops. The excitement and curiosity I saw in people's eyes is unforgettable. It became clear to me that AI is not just a tool for efficiency but a catalyst for inspiration and creativity. This experience reaffirmed my belief in the transformative power of technology when used thoughtfully and ethically.

As you embark on this journey of integrating AI into your teaching practices, I hope you find the same sense of wonder and possibility that I did. Remember, the goal is not to replace the invaluable human elements but to augment them, creating richer and more meaningful learning experiences for our students.

Thank you for joining me on this transformative journey. Let's continue to innovate, inspire, and empower through AI-powered pedagogy. Together, we can redefine education and make a lasting impact on the future of learning.

REFERENCES AND FURTHER READING

3 ways AI can help farmers tackle the challenges of modern agriculture. (n.d.). Retrieved 13 May 2024, from https://theconversation.com/3-ways-ai-can-help-farmers-tackle-the-challenges-of-modern-agriculture-213210

78 Artificial Intelligence Statistics and Trends for 2024. (n.d.). Semrush Blog. Retrieved 7 May 2024, from https://www.semrush.com/blog/artificial-intelligence-stats/

AI and education: Guidance for policy-makers—UNESCO Digital Library. (n.d.). Retrieved 13 May 2024, from https://unesdoc.unesco.org/ark:/48223/pf0000376709

AI at Work Is Here. Now Comes the Hard Part. (n.d.). Retrieved 10 May 2024, from https://www.microsoft.com/en-us/worklab/work-trend-index/ai-at-work-is-here-now-comes-the-hard-part

AI-Principles Overview—OECD.AI. (n.d.). Retrieved 13 May 2024, from https://oecd.ai/en/ai-principles

AIVA, the AI Music Generation Assistant. (n.d.). Retrieved 20 May 2024, from https://www.aiva.ai/

Almulla, M. A. (2020). The Effectiveness of the Project-Based Learning (PBL) Approach as a Way to Engage Students in Learning. *Sage Open*, *10*(3), 2158244020938702. https://doi.org/10.1177/2158244020938702

Asilomar AI Principles. (n.d.). *Future of Life Institute*. Retrieved 22 May 2024, from https://futureoflife.org/open-letter/ai-principles/

BBC Verify | Latest News & Updates | BBC News. (n.d.). Retrieved 9 May 2024, from https://www.bbc.com/news/reality_check

CRAAP test. (2024). In *Wikipedia*. https://en.wikipedia.org/w/index.php?title=CRAAP_test&oldid=121835 0705

CRAAP Test—Evaluating Resources and Misinformation—Library Guides at UChicago. (n.d.). Retrieved 16 May 2024, from https://guides.lib.uchicago.edu/c.php?g=1241077&p=9082343

cycles, T. text provides general information S. assumes no liability for the information given being complete or correct D. to varying update, & Text, S. C. D. M. up-to-D. D. T. R. in the. (n.d.). *Topic: Artificial intelligence (AI) in labor and productivity*. Statista. Retrieved 7 May 2024, from https://www.statista.com/topics/11516/artificial-intelligence-ai-in-labor-and-productivity/

Economic potential of generative AI | McKinsey. (n.d.). Retrieved 7 May 2024, from https://www.mckinsey.com/capabilities/mckinsey-digital/our-insights/the-economic-potential-of-generative-ai-the-next-productivity-frontier#introduction

Ethical impact assessment: A tool of the Recommendation on the Ethics of Artificial Intelligence—UNESCO Digital Library. (n.d.). Retrieved 12 May 2024, from https://unesdoc.unesco.org/ark:/48223/pf0000386276

Ethics guidelines for trustworthy AI | Shaping Europe's digital future. (2019, April 8). https://digital-strategy.ec.europa.eu/en/library/ethics-guidelines-trustworthy-ai

Evaluating Sources: CARRDSS. (n.d.). H-B Woodlawn. Retrieved 15 May 2024, from https://hbwoodlawn.apsva.us/library-home/research/evaluating-resources-caardss/

FactCheck.org. (n.d.). FactCheck.Org. Retrieved 9 May 2024, from
https://www.factcheck.org/

Family Educational Rights and Privacy Act (FERPA). (n.d.). Retrieved 17 May
2024, from
https://www2.ed.gov/policy/gen/guid/fpco/ferpa/index.html

Family Educational Rights and Privacy Act (FERPA). (2021, August 25).
[Guides]. US Department of Education (ED).
https://www2.ed.gov/policy/gen/guid/fpco/ferpa/index.html

Gemini – chat to supercharge your ideas. (n.d.). Gemini. Retrieved 15 May
2024, from https://gemini.google.com

General Data Protection Regulation (GDPR) – Legal Text. (n.d.). General
Data Protection Regulation (GDPR). Retrieved 17 May 2024, from
https://gdpr-info.eu/

Google Scholar. (n.d.). Retrieved 9 May 2024, from
https://scholar.google.com/

Guy, I. R., Jack. (2023, October 2). *Tom Hanks says dental plan video uses
'AI version of me' without permission.* CNN.
https://www.cnn.com/2023/10/02/entertainment/tom-hanks-ai-
dental-plan-video-intl-scli/index.html

Hardman, D. P. (2024, January 11). AI & "Un-Personalised" Learning
[Substack newsletter]. *Dr Phil's Newsletter, Powered by DOMS™ A.*
https://drphilippahardman.substack.com/p/un-personalised-
learning

How could AI change life on farms and estates? (n.d.). Strutt & Parker -
Rural Hub. Retrieved 13 May 2024, from
https://rural.struttandparker.com/article/how-could-ai-change-life-
in-the-rural-sector/

Is AI-Generated Content Actually Detectable? (2024, April 23). College of
Computer, Mathematical, and Natural Sciences | University of

Maryland. https://cmns.umd.edu/news-events/news/ai-generated-content-actually-detectable

Is Prompt Engineering Really Prompt 'Engineering'? (n.d.). Jennifer Chang Wathall. Retrieved 2 May 2024, from https://www.jenniferchangwathall.com/single-post/is-prompt-engineering-really-prompt-engineering

Kampen, K. V. (n.d.). *Library Guides: Evaluating Resources and Misinformation: CRAAP Test*. Retrieved 16 May 2024, from https://guides.lib.uchicago.edu/c.php?g=1241077&p=9082343

Kurt, D. S. (2023). SAMR Model: Substitution, Augmentation, Modification, and Redefinition. *Educational Technology*. https://educationaltechnology.net/samr-model-substitution-augmentation-modification-and-redefinition/

Lu, J. (n.d.). *Research Guides: Artificial Intelligence (AI): How to Cite AI Generated Content*. Retrieved 9 May 2024, from https://guides.lib.purdue.edu/c.php?g=1371380&p=10135074

Marcus. (2024, February 12). The 15 Most Common ChatGPT Phrases. *AI Phrase Finder*. https://aiphrasefinder.com/common-chatgpt-phrases/

PDPC | Singapore's Approach to AI Governance. (n.d.). Retrieved 21 November 2023, from https://www.pdpc.gov.sg/Help-and-Resources/2020/01/Model-AI-Governance-Framework

Polger, M. A. (n.d.). *CSI Library: Misinformation and Disinformation: Thinking Critically about Information Sources: Web Sites for Fact Checking*. Retrieved 9 May 2024, from https://library.csi.cuny.edu/c.php?g=619342&p=4310783

PolitiFact. (n.d.). Retrieved 9 May 2024, from https://www.politifact.com/

PricewaterhouseCoopers. (n.d.). *2024 AI Business Predictions*. PwC. Retrieved 7 May 2024, from https://www.pwc.com/us/en/tech-effect/ai-analytics/ai-predictions.html

Project-Based Learning (PBL). (n.d.). Edutopia. Retrieved 20 May 2024, from https://www.edutopia.org/project-based-learning

Recommendation on the Ethics of Artificial Intelligence—UNESCO Digital Library. (n.d.). Retrieved 20 November 2023, from https://unesdoc.unesco.org/ark:/48223/pf0000381137

ResearchRabbit. (n.d.). ResearchRabbit. Retrieved 23 May 2024, from https://www.researchrabbit.ai

scheme=AGLSTERMS. AglsAgent; corporateName=Department of Education; address=50 Marcus Clarke St, C. C. (2023, December 1). *The Australian Framework for Generative Artificial Intelligence (AI) in Schools* [Text]. scheme=AGLSTERMS.AglsAgent; corporateName=Department of Education; address=50 Marcus Clarke St, Canberra City, ACT 2601; contact=+61 1300 566 046. https://www.education.gov.au/schooling/announcements/australian -framework-generative-artificial-intelligence-ai-schools

Scite Assistant—Your AI Research Partner. (n.d.). Scite.Ai. Retrieved 23 May 2024, from https://scite.ai

TED (Director). (2024, April 23). *What Is an AI Anyway? | Mustafa Suleyman | TED*. https://www.youtube.com/watch?v=KKNCiRWd_j0

The AI Classroom: The Ultimate Guide to Artificial Intelligence in Education (The Everything Edtech Series): 9781959419112: Fitzpatrick, Dan, Fox, Amanda, Weinstein, Brad: Books. (n.d.). Retrieved 2 May 2024, from https://www.amazon.com/Classroom-Artificial-Intelligence-Education-Hitchhikers/dp/1959419110

The importance of academic integrity: Q&A with IB Academic Integrity Manager, Celina Garza—Part one | IB Community Blog. (n.d.). Retrieved 21 November 2023, from https://blogs.ibo.org/2022/05/16/the-importance-of-academic-integrity-qa-with-ib-academic-integrity-manager-celina-garza-part-one/

The most overused ChatGPT words—Plus. (n.d.). Retrieved 3 May 2024, from https://www.plusdocs.com/blog/the-most-overused-chatgpt-words

The power of inquiry: Teaching and learning with curiosity, creativity and purpose in the contemporary classroom: Kath Murdoch: 9780975841211: Amazon.com: Books. (n.d.). Retrieved 17 May 2024, from https://www.amazon.com/power-inquiry-curiosity-creativity-contemporary/dp/0975841211

The state of AI in 2023: Generative AI's breakout year | McKinsey. (n.d.). Retrieved 4 May 2024, from https://www.mckinsey.com/capabilities/quantumblack/our-insights/the-state-of-ai-in-2023-generative-ais-breakout-year

UN Human Rights (Director). (2017, May 15). *Universal Declaration of Human Rights.* https://www.youtube.com/watch?v=5RR4VXNX3jA

Weber-Wulff, D., Anohina-Naumeca, A., Bjelobaba, S., Foltýnek, T., Guerrero-Dib, J., Popoola, O., Šigut, P., & Waddington, L. (2023). Testing of Detection Tools for AI-Generated Text. *International Journal for Educational Integrity, 19*(1), 26. https://doi.org/10.1007/s40979-023-00146-z

What is PBL? (n.d.). PBLWorks. Retrieved 20 May 2024, from https://www.pblworks.org/what-is-pbl

APPENDIX A
TOP 50 AI TOOLS
(AS OF MAY 2024)

10 AI Image/ Video Generators

Adobe Firefly: **Image Generator** https://www.adobe.com/hk_en/products/firefly.html	Adobe Firefly, a product of Adobe Creative Cloud, is a generative machine learning model that is used in the field of design.
Canva Magic Studio: **Image and Video** **generator** https://www.canva.com/magic/	Canva is an online design and visual communication platform free for all educators
DALL·E 3 Image Generator https://openai.com/index/dall-e-3/	DALL·E 3 understands significantly more nuance and detail than our previous systems, allowing you to easily translate your ideas into exceptionally accurate images.
HeyGen—Video Generator https://www.heygen.com	HeyGen is an online tool that helps you generate or repurpose videos using AI technologies include digital avatars, text-to-video, and video translations.
Lumen5— Video Generator https://lumen5.com/	Lumen5 is a video creation platform powered by AI that enables anyone without training or

	experience to easily create engaging video content within minutes.
Pictory— Video Generator https://pictory.ai/	Pictory's powerful AI enables you to create and edit professional quality videos using text, no technical skills required or software to download.
Scribble Diffusion: Image Generator https://scribblediffusion.com/	Turn your sketch into a refined image using AI
Shutterstock: AI Image Generator https://www.shutterstock.com/ai-image-generator	The best AI image generator is easy-to-use & ready to convert your text prompts into innovative AI photos in hundreds of creative AI art styles in seconds.
Stability AI: Image Generator https://stability.ai	Activating humanity's potential through generative AI. Open models in every modality, for everyone, everywhere.
Stable Diffusion XL: Image Generator https://stablediffusionxl.com/	Stable Diffusion XL or SDXL is the latest image generation model that is tailored towards more photorealistic outputs with more detailed imagery and

11 LLMs

ChatGPT including GPT-4o and GPT4o-128k https://chatgpt.com	A conversational AI system that listens, learns, and challenges. The latest GPT-4omni is multimodal
ChatPDF - Chat with any PDF https://www.chatpdf.com/?ref=aieducator.tools	ChatPDF is the fast and easy way to chat with any PDF, free and without sign-in. Talk to books, research papers, manuals, essays, legal contracts, whatever you have! The intelligence revolution is here, ChatGPT was just the beginning!
Character.ai -Personalized AI for every moment of your day. https://character.ai/	Meet AIs that feel alive. Chat with anyone, anywhere, anytime. Experience the power of super-intelligent chat bots that hear you, understand you, and remember you.
Claude: Haiku, Sonnet, and Opus from Anthropic. https://claude.ai/login?returnTo=%2F%3F	*Claude 3 is the latest and most advanced version of Anthropic's AI language model, released in March 2024. It consists of three models - (the most powerful), with capabilities like multimodal understanding of text and images*
Gemini Pro from Google https://deepmind.google/technologies/gemini/pro/	*Gemini Pro 1.5 is a powerful multimodal AI model developed by Google that can process and understand various types of data, including text, images, audio, and video.*
Magic To Do—GoblinTools https://goblin.tools/	*Breaking things down so you don't!* *Goblin.tools is a collection of small, simple, single-task tools, mostly designed to help neurodivergent people with tasks they find overwhelming or difficult.*
Microsoft Bing: Your Everyday AI Companion https://www.microsoft.com/en-gb/bing	*Learn how to access and use Copilot to tap into the impressive power, productivity, and creativity of AI chat.*

Perplexity https://www.perplexity.ai/	*Perplexity is an AI-powered search engine and chatbot that uses natural language processing (NLP) and machine learning to provide answers to user queries. It's designed to search the web in real-time and provide up-to-date information on various topics.*
Pi, your personal AI https://pi.ai/talk	*Pi is a free AI chatbot that provides factual and emotional support. It's designed to be conversational and understand natural language, and it can be used to ask questions, chat, and organize thinking.*
Poe https://poe.com/	*Poe AI provides access to a wide range of AI chatbots from leading developers like OpenAI and Anthropic. The AI on Poe is powered by models from several sources, including:OpenAI: ChatGPT, GPT-4, and DALL-E 3* *Anthropic: Claude Instant and Claude 2* *Stability AI: Stable DiffusionXL* *Google: PaLM and Gemini-Pro* *Meta: Llama 2 to name a few.*
Upword—AI powered research and knowledge assistant. https://www.upword.ai/	*Organize your life's content, ask your AI assistant anything, conduct research with AI superpowers, create personalized summary docs, and manage your knowledge for life.*

14 Education Specific

Book Creator—Love Learning https://bookcreator.com/	*Book Creator is the simplest, most inclusive way to create content in the classroom.*
Brisk Teaching | AI Tools for Teachers. https://www.briskteaching.com/ ai-tools-for-teachers	*30+ time-saving AI tools for teachers! Brisk is a Chrome extension, filled with magic AI tools that streamline your teaching prep. Teachers use Brisk to save time where they are already working - in Google Docs, Slides, YouTube, articles, and more. Brisk automates grading, feedback, and interactive lesson planning to optimize teacher workflows and enhance student learning outcomes.*
Canva free for educators https://www.canva.com/ education/	*Canva is an online design and visual communication platform free for all educators*
Curipod https://curipod.com/	*Curipod makes interactive lessons filled with creativity, reflection and critical thinking*
Diffit https://web.diffit.me/	*Teachers use Diffit to get "just right" instructional materials, saving tons of time and helping all students to access grade level content*
Edpuzzle | Make Any Video Your Lesson. https://edpuzzle.com/ ?ref=aieducator.tools	*Easily create beautiful interactive video lessons for your students you can integrate right into your LMS. Track students' progress with hassle-free analytics as you flip your classroom!*
Eduaide.Ai: Instruction by Design. https://www.eduaide.ai/	*Eduaide.Ai is an AI-driven platform that helps educators create lesson plans, teaching resources, and assessments.*
Education Copilot: AI Lesson Planner	*Generate AI lesson plans, PowerPoints, and more with Copilot! Use Copilot to breeze*

https://educationcopilot.com/	through your unit planning and material creation!
MagicSchool.ai https://www.magicschool.ai/	Educators use MagicSchool to help lesson plan, differentiate, write assessments, write IEPs, communicate clearly, and more.
Padlet https://padlet.com/dashboard	Make beautiful collaborative boards to collect, organize, and present anything.
ParentSquare https://www.parentsquare.com/about/	School and Parent Communication They are passionate about better connecting schools with families to improve student outcomes.
Parlay Ideas https://parlayideas.com/	Parlay is an AI-powered instructional platform that helps teachers facilitate meaningful, measurable, and inclusive class discussions
PhET Interactive Simulations (Technically not AI but great ed tech!) https://phet.colorado.edu/	Founded in 2002 by Nobel Laureate Carl Wieman, the PhET Interactive Simulations project at the University of Colorado Boulder creates free interactive math and science simulations. PhET sims are based on extensive research and engage students through an intuitive, game-like environment where students learn through exploration and discovery.
Would You Rather Question Generator | Auto Classmate https://autoclassmate.io/tools/would-you-rather-question-generator/	This AI tool will instantly add excitement to your classroom by providing grade and content specific 'would you rather' style questions.

6 Writing and Grammar

AI-Writer.com™—AI Text Generator https://ai-writer.com/	AI-Writer focuses on researching and writing, seo-focused text, editor verifiable citations, and text rewording to name a few
Grammarly: Free AI Writing Assistance. https://www.grammarly.com/	*Offer spelling, punctuation, grammar, and style corrections as you type.*
Merlin AI | Ask AI to Research, Write, Summarize in 1-click https://www.getmerlin.in	*Free AI Chat to answer all your queries. Ask AI to summarize videos, articles, pdf, and websites, write emails, content on social media, and review content using AI detector.*
ProWritingAid https://prowritingaid.com/product-focused-homepage	*Great writing made easy. Your personal writing coach. A grammar checker, style editor, and writing mentor in one package.*
QuillBot AI: Paraphrasing Tool https://quillbot.com/	*QuillBot is a software developed in 2017 that uses artificial intelligence to rewrite and paraphrase text.*
Quill.org | Interactive Writing and Grammar. https://www.quill.org/	*Quill provides free writing and grammar activities for middle and high school students.*

4 Research Tools

Consensus: AI Search Engine for Research. https://consensus.app/	*ChatGPT for Research. Consensus is an AI-powered search engine that finds and summarizes scientific research papers. Just ask a question!*
NewsGPT https://newsgpt.ai/about-us/	*NewsGPT delivers unbiased news, powered by AI-generated articles that eliminate personal opinions, ensuring transparency and impartial information*
ResearchRabbit https://www.researchrabbit.ai	*The most powerful discovery app ever built for researchers*
Scite Assistant—Your AI Research Partner https://scite.ai	*Researchers around the world use Scite to better understand research, uncover debates, ensure they are citing reliable studies, and improve their writing.*

5 Miscellaneous

Miro Assist | Miro https://miro.com/assist/	*Using Design Principles* *You're here to create the next big thing and we're here to help. Unlock the power of your ideas with Miro Assist – your new launchpad for creativity, collaboration, and productivity.*
Mubert—Thousands of Staff-Picked Royalty-Free Music Tracks for Streaming, Videos, Podcasts, Commercial Use and Online Content. https://mubert.com/	*Mubert - The new royalty-free music ecosystem for content creators, brands and developers Come See How Our High-Quality Music Can Elevate Your Content*
Mural AI: Meet your new teammate https://www.mural.co/ai	*Experience a better way to work with Mural AI and Mural's Microsoft 365 Copilot integration. Improve collaboration, explore new ideas, and take your teams to new heights of productivity and innovation.*
MusicFX from Google https://aitestkitchen.withgoogle.com/tools/music-fx	*Google's MusicFX is a new language model that can convert text descriptions into audio clips.*
Numerous.ai https://numerous.ai/	Elevate your spreadsheet work with our Spreadsheet *AI* Tool, integrating ChatGPT intelligence through *AI* for Excel and *AI* for Google Sheets plugins.

Made in the USA
Las Vegas, NV
26 November 2024